6-13-06 (c)

B.C.

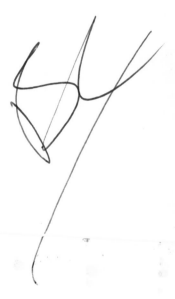

# WOMEN AND WORSHIP

# WOMEN
## AND
# WORSHIP

*A Guide to Nonsexist Hymns,*
*Prayers, and Liturgies*

### REVISED AND EXPANDED EDITION

## Sharon Neufer Emswiler
## Thomas Neufer Emswiler

*1817*

**Harper & Row, Publishers, San Francisco**

Cambridge, Hagerstown, New York, Philadelphia
London, Mexico City, São Paulo, Sydney

*Designer: Jim Mennick*

Library of Congress Cataloging in Publication Data

Emswiler, Sharon Neufer.
    WOMEN AND WORSHIP.

    Bibliography: p.
    1. Sexism in liturgical language. 2. Liturgies. I. Neufer Emswiler, Tom, DATE. II. Title.
BV178.N48    1984    264    83–48459
ISBN 0-06-066101-1

84   85   86   87   88   10   9   8   7   6   5   4   3   2   1

*To all those who are struggling
to make the liberating presence of Christ
more real in our churches*

# Contents

# Preface to the Revised Edition

Shortly after we had written *Women and Worship* we were leading a workshop on sexist language. We had made our presentations, generated much dialogue, and concluded with a brief worship service. Afterward people came up to talk with us. One woman made a comment I have never forgotten.

"I see you have chosen your life's vocation," she said.

I was taken aback by her statement.

"You don't mean that you expect we'll be leading workshops like this for the rest of our lives?"

"I most certainly do," she said.

I must admit that I went into the concern for sexist language naively. I thought all we had to do was write our book explaining clearly and logically the problems with such language in worship and everyone would see the light. At most it might take two or three years for the change to occur.

But I have begun to see that the woman at our workshop was wiser. Change in language and worship is not easy. It takes much persistence and sometimes quite a bit of time for people to "see the light."

But the light is beginning to dawn. Ten years after our book, which was the first to deal with sexist language and worship, many other resources have been produced. Part of the purpose of this new edition is to examine some of these other resources and make recommendations. Changes are occurring in other ways too. Almost every mainline denomination now has a task force at work on inclusive language. Changes in church school curriculum, magazine and book editorial departments, and worship resources are happening. Honest efforts are being made to grapple with the problems of sexist language in the Church.

Even on the grass roots level we see much more openness to these issues than ten years ago. When we first led workshops around the country we had to spend most of our time explaining why this issue was important and working through all the negative reactions to changes in language and liturgy. Now we find almost everywhere we go that most people have already been thinking about this issue and have ideas to share about what to do. Most are quite sympathetic to concerns about sexist language as it is used for people. Many still have much thinking to do when it comes to sexist language about God. But there *is* a dramatic shift toward wanting to do something about sexist language in worship.

However, these positive comments must be balanced against reports of our visits to local churches where it often seems as if this issue had never surfaced. Part of the problem is the lag between new consciousness and old worship resources. We have many practical suggestions in this revised edition to help overcome this lag, but the reality of sexist language and practice is still much with us in most of our churches. Thus the woman who told us that we had chosen our life vocation when we became concerned about sexist language may well have been right. I see continuing work ahead at all levels from national policy groups to small clusters of pastors and lay people. And the progress that has been made thus far convinces me that justice will finally prevail through hard work, prayers, and the care of an increasing number of people.

I would be remiss if I did not add a personal note in this preface about how language concerns have affected me as a middle-class male in the United States today. The change that has come into my life as a result of wrestling with language problems is immense. It has not only sensitized me to the concerns of women but also to those of many other oppressed groups. The revolution in language that I have experienced in my talk about God has had more influence on the growth of my theological understanding than any other factor. It has deepened my theological insight and my spiritual life. Although the journey into language has not been without pain, it is a journey that I feel fortunate to have begun and that I am glad to continue to be on.

TOM NEUFER EMSWILER

\*     \*     \*

When I first became aware of the problem of sexism in language I felt very much alone. I knew that there was something very wrong with a language that excluded women from its structure in obvious ways. I knew it was a strong political statement when the English language identified the male as the norm, the standard, the real human being, but it seemed as though very few people cared about this problem, or even recognized it. Whenever the issue was raised, especially in large groups of people, the most common response was laughter.

Today, for the most part, the laughter has died away. The issue is taken seriously and those actively promoting it are a serious force to be reckoned with. The most gratifying aspect of the language issue for me in the past ten years has been the increasing numbers of people who have had their eyes and ears opened to the sexism within the English language and have determined to do something about it. It has been very satisfying to see the mainline denominations respond in positive ways through task forces, guidelines, and recommendations concerning nonsexist language. I no longer feel alone. Instead I feel the company and support of women and men who are working hard to eliminate sexism from the language of the Church and from the English language wherever it is used.

At the same time, it is discouraging and disappointing for me to attend worship in a church or be with a group of pastors who seem totally oblivious to the reality of sexist language and the power it has in our lives. I believe that concern about sexist language has been with us long enough now that pastors, especially, should be aware of it and should be at least in the process of struggling with it in their worship services. This is the point at which the woman Tom mentioned earlier knew what she was talking about. We still have a long way to go and it is not yet time to sit back and relax. It is in the hope that this book may help to increase awareness and help in the practical matters of language use that we offer this revised edition of *Women and Worship*.

SHARON NEUFER EMSWILER

# Introduction

This book grew out of pain and hope. The pain belongs to women who have begun to discover that for centuries they have been forced to receive their identity from men rather than from God. The hope is that women are beginning to break free from their bondage to subservient roles as they discover the profound potential within them. For those of use who call ourselves Christians, this new freedom must find expression in our worship. If it does not, our worship is no longer an honest presentation of what we believe about life, and increasing numbers of women and men will find themselves alienated from all that the traditional Church stands for.

This book was written to try to provide guidelines for those who wish to learn how to develop creative, meaningful nonsexist worship. It is intended not just for the concerned minister or professional worship leader but also for lay women and men who want to participate actively in changing attitudes of worship in their churches.

In order to deal most responsibly with this subject, we have made several assumptions about you, the reader. We assume that you are at least mildly concerned about the importance of language in worship. We also assume that you hope that the language of worship can be redesigned in such a way as to bring maximum meaning to as many people as possible. Further, we assume that you have noticed or had called to your attention that much of the language used in worship services is sexist, that is, it is heavily overloaded with masculine references—"brother," "sons of God," "mankind," and so forth. Finally, we are assuming that you want to do something about this sexism.

If, however, you are not sure whether you should bother to try to do something about sexist worship, read Chapter 1. You'll discover how painfully offensive most worship is today to women who are struggling to discover their unique humanness in a male-dominated world.

If you recognize the reality of sexism within most worship but are "hung up" on the theological and historical arguments regarding the validity of substituting new language, you should read Chapters 2 through 4. Chapter 2 explores what we know about language from theology as well as psychology, sociology, and linguistics. Chapter 3 will help you to discover that the basic biblical witness offers a clear mandate to those of us who wish to develop a new way of talking about the faith. Chapter 4 will help you to see that a "god" encased in male-dominated language is too small to be GOD and that our understanding of God can be expanded as we are able to see beyond male and female images.

The "how-to" portions of this book begin with Chapter 5. Here and in the following chapters we attempt to share with you examples of our own attempts to liberate liturgy.

Also it is important for you to recognize that in this book we are not attempting to present a complete theology of worship. Many other books, such as *New Forms of Worship* by James F. White and *The Future Present* by Marianne H. Micks, already do this job admirably. Our emphasis here is on giving you practical concepts and examples so that you will be able to take a form of worship you can already justify theologically and change it so it is no longer sexist.

This book is, of course, only a beginning. It represents where we are on our own journey toward a new consciousness and creative liturgy. Our hope is that you can take some of our ideas and use them to begin to "redeem" your local situation with your own creative, nonsexist liturgy.

# 1. How the New Woman Feels in the Old Worship Service

## SHARON NEUFER EMSWILER

Worship is at the very heart of the Christian life. It is the pulsating center from which we receive God's love and strength for all that we are and do. Like the blood that flows through our bodies, we keep returning to that heart for refreshment and renewal. But what happens when the heart fails to function correctly? For an increasing number of women the heart of our lives as Christians is no longer providing the meaning and power we so desperately need. Why is this so? Perhaps the best way to answer this question is for me to describe my feelings as a woman participating in an average worship service.

I enter the sanctuary and am directed to my seat by an usher, always male, except on "Ladies' Day," that one day in the year when women are given the opportunity to "play usher." As I sit and meditate I listen to the organ prelude. If the church is a small one, I notice that the organist is a woman. However, if the church is a large, prestigious one, with an expensive organ, the position of organist is most often filled by a man.

The minister (or ministers)—male, of course—then appears to begin the service, accompanied by a lay person (male) acting as the liturgist of the morning. The call to worship is given, setting the worship service in motion. One such call to worship that sticks in my mind from a service I attended contains the line, "To be is to be a brother." Hearing those words, I instantly carry them to their logical conclusion: "I am not, and never will be, a brother. Therefore, I am not. I do not exist." The service is off to a great start!

The congregation now rises for the first hymn and I find myself singing a song such as "Men and Children Everywhere" (I wonder in which group I am to include myself), "Rise Up, O Men of God," or "Faith of Our Fathers." If it is near Christmas, the selections might be "God Rest Ye, Merry Gentlemen" or Good Christian Men, Rejoice"; while the Easter season offers such choices as "Sing with All the Sons of Glory" or "Good Christian Men Rejoice and Sing." Other possible hymns in the service might include "Once to Every Man and Nation," "Now Praise We Great and Famous Men," "Brother Man, Fold to Thy Heart," "As Men of Old Their First Fruits Brought," or "Turn Back, O Man."

If the service is of a more contemporary style, I go in the hope that the hymns will speak to me in a way that the traditional ones do not. But here, too, I am asked to sing songs with titles like "Be a New Man," "Sons of God," "Come, My Brothers," "Brothers, Get Yourselves Together," and "Brother, How's Your Love."

As I sing I try to imagine that these songs are speaking to me, but I am not accustomed to thinking of myself as a "man" or a "brother"; the identification is difficult, and most often impossible. The only way I can find to identify with these masculine words is to attempt either to deny or set aside my femininity. But I do not want to deny that part of my personhood; I want rather to affirm it. I want my femaleness recognized and affirmed by the Church also. As the worship progresses through the prayers, creeds, and sermon, the same language form keeps recurring—always the masculine when referring to people; always the masculine when referring to God. While I sing and during prayer I change the word "men" to "people," "mankind" to "humankind," "sons" to "children," "Father" to "Parent," but I feel as though I am outshouted by the rest of the congregation. My words are swallowed up by theirs.

Listening to the minister preach his sermon for the morning, I am aware that he is not really attempting to address me or my sisters in the congregation. His illustrations all revolve around men and speak overwhelmingly to the masculine experience in our society. Suddenly, I feel as though I am eavesdropping on a conversation labeled "For Men Only." Or worse yet, I feel that the suspicion I had after the call to worship is true. I do not exist! I look down at my hands and arms and feet. I can see them; they are very real to me. But I feel that somehow I must be invisible to this preacher who has designed this service and now stands in front of me, speaking of "the brethren" and telling his congregation to be "new men."

Following the sermon, the worshippers are invited to participate in the celebration of the Lord's Supper. As the large group of male ushers marches down the aisle to receive the communion elements and distribute them to the congregation, I am suddenly struck with the irony of the situation. The chicken suppers, the ham suppers, the turkey suppers in the church are all prepared and served by the women. But not the Lord's Supper! Yes, it is prepared by the women, but the privilege of serving the Lord's Supper in worship is reserved for the men. This particular morning I find it very difficult to swallow the bread and drink the wine, knowing that within the Body of Christ, the Church, the sisters of Christ are not given the same respect and privileges as are his brothers.

By this point in the service I am feeling extremely uneasy, almost as though I am suffocating. I want very much for the hour to come to an end so that I can run to the door and breathe the fresh air. Then I will know once again that I do exist, that I am alive, that I am not invisible.

When the worship hour is concluded I leave the church wondering, "Why am I going away feeling less human than when I came?" That which should have created a sense of wholeness in me made me feel dehumanized, less than a full person. What was meant to be a time of worship of the true God was, for me, a worship of the masculine—the masculine experience among humans and the masculine dimension of God.

In yet other ways male leadership in the worship of most of the larger mainline denominations reflects what society believes to be masculine. The worship in these churches is reasoned, intellectual, and often cold, lacking the emotional warmth and spontaneity more common to the feminine experience. When the presence and participation of women is reflected in the liturgy or in the sermon, it is done in a patronizing and condescending manner, assuming stereotyped roles for us in the family, Church, and society. Women are not recognized as mature adults with abilities and interests as great and varied as those of men.

I know that I am not alone in my reactions to most Christian worship services. On occasions when I have been leading the liturgy in a worship service and have included the appropriate feminine word along with the masculine one that is written in the liturgy, women have often expressed their appreciation. They are pleased that someone has recognized their presence.

For me, the most momentous occasion showing women's feeling toward the total use of masculine terminology in worship was a service in which all of the participants were women and all the words for humans and for God were feminine. At first we felt rather silly and somewhat rebellious substituting "sisterhood" for "brotherhood" and "she" for "he" when speaking of God. But as we moved through the service the mood began to change to seriousness and excitement, reaching a climax at the conclusion of the Scripture reading in which it was said that God's covenant was given to "Sarah and her daughters." The women received those words with spontaneous applause and joyous laughter. Never before had I heard that kind of response to a Scripture reading! It was as though we women were hearing those words for the very first time in our lives. God's promise extended to *us*, the daughters of the faith.

If you are a man reading this and still are not convinced of the need for more inclusive terms in our liturgical language, or if you are a woman who has not experienced any difficulty with the predominance of masculine words, try this experiment: Turn to 1 John 2:9–11 and read it aloud. Now read it aloud again substituting the appropriate feminine word every time a masculine word is given. Do you *feel* any difference in your reaction to that passage when using feminine terminology? Do you, as a man, feel as close to the meaning of that passage when reading it the second time? Do you, as a woman, feel closer or further from it when using the feminine words? Try the same experiment with other books, particularly ones that use the generic "man" in abundance as do most theology books.

The words we use in worship are important also because of the *images* they form in our minds. When we hear the word "man" or "brother" or "son," the image in our mind is most often a masculine image rather than a feminine one. Because these same words are used in reference to the male specific as well as the generic, the masculine becomes much more closely associated with it in our minds. Therefore, the tendency is to form a masculine image when hearing a statement such as "If any *man* is in Christ, *he* is a new creature." The image most of us form is likely to be of a male "man" rather than a female "man." Because the masculine is the image we carry in relation to that word "man," we subconsciously receive a different message than the one actually intended, a message much more closely tied to the male than to the female human being. When a male or female is constantly bombarded with masculine terminology and masculine imagery, the result is to form the conclusion, unconsciously, that all life is lived in the masculine gender, by the male sex, thus placing the female outside the boundaries of *human* life, in a world of her own. This conclusion is strengthened by the fact that the words for the male specific, "man," and the words "human" or "human being" are interchangeable; thus woman stands apart from human.

Another problem raised by using "man" and "men" to denote both males and females is that the woman is not sure when she is supposed to be included and when she is not. Sometimes the context of the statement is a clue. "We need some men to help move the pulpit and lectern following the service this morning," most likely means "males." "All mankind is one brotherhood" probably is intended to include women as well. However, statements like "All men are created equal" and "God calls men to the ministry" leave some question in our minds. "All men are created equal" is *said* to include women but in practice is often interpreted to mean "all males." "God calls men to the ministry" leaves a woman wondering whether women are not called or whether at this particular moment she is to consider herself and all women as "men." The perceptive woman soon discovers that while she has been told that "man" generically used includes her, in practice it is often interpreted to mean "Males Only." The ambiguity of the terms allows women to think they are included while in reality they often are definitely excluded.

Language has a powerful influence on our lives; it is not a trivial matter. Words form the bridges from one human being to another. We must always strive to see that these bridges go where we want them to go and that they are kept in good repair. When words no longer communicate what we thought they did or what we want them to communicate, it is time to use other words or even create new ones to express ourselves. This is what the Church is being called to do in the language of its worship.

# 2. The Importance of Language: Witness from Theology, Psychology, Sociology, and Linguistics

We became sensitized to the importance of language through our own personal experience of its power in our lives. Its power and significance is underlined when we examine biblical theology and when we study contemporary psychology, sociology, and linguistics. In this chapter we propose to do both.

## Biblical Theology: Its Witness to the Importance of Language

Ours is a theology of the word. We read in Genesis that God created with the word. Again and again creation happens when we hear the words "And God said." The writer of Genesis knew intuitively that creation begins with an idea and that ideas are most often formed by means of words. Things take on a new reality once spoken. And when they are named, a relationship is created between the one named and the one naming. So God asks Adam (Hebrew for "humankind") to name all the rest of creation, giving Adam by that act of inventing and using words a responsibility toward the rest of creation.

The significance of the word continues in biblical thought. John especially likes this concept and tells us that "in the beginning was the Word and the Word was with God and the Word was God.'' The Word is made manifest, we are told, in Jesus Christ.

The Bible is often called the Word of God. Actually, it is Jesus Christ who is the Word; the Bible is words telling us about the Word. But the fact that the word concept is identified with the Bible simply underlines again how crucial language has been to the development of our faith understandings. The fact that the primary revelation of our faith, Jesus Christ, is called the Word is the most telling evidence for importance of language in our faith.

And Jesus took the power of words with utmost seriousness. In the Sermon on the Mount, he says that we must not heap up empty phrases in our prayers but simply say what we really mean (Matt. 6:7). He also insists that we simplify our language and be as clear as possible in what we mean. He would have none of the rigamarole of fancy oaths that was popular in his day. He says that, instead, we should simply say a clear yes or no in making agreements (Matt. 5:33 ff.).

Jesus' most forceful and striking reference to the power of language came in his battle with the scribes and the Pharisees. Angered by their hypocrisy, he says:

> You brood of vipers! how can you speak good, when you are evil? For out of the abundance of the heart the mouth speaks. Good people out of their treasure bring forth good, and evil people out of their evil treasure bring forth evil. I tell you, on the day of judgment people will render account for every careless word they utter; for *by your words you will be judged, and by your words you will be condemned.* (Matt. 12:34–37; italics ours, paraphrase ours.)

Not only is the heart of the Christian faith called the Word, but the founding and maintaining of the Church is wrapped up in two events dealing with language. In the Tower of Babel story (Gen. 11:1–9) we have a beautiful parable showing how language can fragment a people. Without common words that all could understand, the people could no longer work together. Pentecost (Acts 2) is a reversal of Babel. Somehow through the power of the Gospel, people who spoke many different languages now understood one another. The Word was made clear to them in this miraculous event and through it came the birth of the Church. Parabolically, although certainly not always actually, the Church is that community where people are brought together again in the common language of God's love.

As the Church developed, the importance of language continued to be emphasized. The "speaking in tongues" controversy that concerns Paul (1 Cor. 14:6 ff.) is basically a concern for clarity in communication. Paul doesn't say "speaking in tongues" is completely wrong, but he does believe that if it is done in public worship, it should be done with some sense of order and propriety and someone should be available to interpret for the whole congregation. Without this interpreter, Pentecost turns back into Babel.

The struggle to communicate with words is also evident in the early efforts of Christ's followers to write down their experiences to share with others. Lexographer Walter Bauer, in the introduction to his Greek lexicon, tells how the early New Testament writers developed new word formations, compounded old words with new, adopted foreign words, and used specialized and technical terms and shifts in grammatical structure all in the effort to communicate more clearly and forcefully. Koine Greek became beautiful, but not without agonizing linguistic adventures by many New Testament writers.

Our entire Church history is a continuing record of struggles to make the Word more accessible and understandable to the people of God. Sometimes this struggle was extremely costly. Many of the early biblical translators who attempted to make the Bible accessible to all by rendering it in the common language of the people faced severe opposition from Church leaders who recognized the great threat of such an effort to their authority. Many of these courageous early translators gave their lives just so words could appear on the pages of books.

The struggle to translate truthfully is still with us. People have recently become aware of the male bias of most translations of the Bible. Almost all translators until recently have been men. They were dealing with a book admittedly out of patriarchal times, but often they produced translations more male biased than the original. Ruth Hoppin in her article "Games Bible Translators Play" (see Appendix C) gives many examples of this tendency. For example, a word that clearly means "children" in Greek has often been translated as "sons" (see John 1:12, KJV).

We are looking forward to the new edition of the Revised Standard Version of the Bible, which will seriously consider the actual meaning of the Greek and Hebrew words as related to sexist language. The purpose of this version is not to paraphrase all sexism out of the texts, but to be as inclusive as is really warranted by the actual Hebrew and Greek words. In this sense, it will be our most accurate translation. We believe there is also a place for paraphrases of the Bible that do eliminate all sexist references to God and people. They can help us hear and understand passages in a new way. *The Word for Us* by Joan Haugerud (see Appendix C) is one such attempt of Mark, John, Romans, and Galatians. Although we wish the author would have felt free to deviate more from the Revised Standard Version in producing a more poetic text, and although we do not always feel she chooses the right words to substitute for old familiar sexisms, still we have been helped by this work and have used it at times both in private meditation and in public worship.

We certainly encourage those persons who have the linguistic skills to develop their own translations and/or paraphrases. Those of us who are not so trained can still do a responsible job of paraphrasing by comparing several different translations and reading several commentaries on a particular passage. When reading a paraphrase in a worship service, it should be stated that a paraphrase is being read, and credit should be given to the author. Reading such paraphrases occasionally in worship is in keeping with our basic concern of sharing the fullness of the Gospel with which the Scripture writers and others down through our history struggled.

## A Brief Linguistic History of Sexist Language

Often when we lead workshops on eliminating sexist language we are accused of "tampering" with the language. We are told that we must leave the language to its "natural development." Changes will then occur spontaneously and language will evolve gradually.

This argument appears somewhat persuasive until we study the history of the English language as related to sexism in some depth. For example, one of the primary sexist problems in our language today is the use of "he" or "man" as generic. To most of us untutored in linguistics, this appears to have developed "naturally" over a long period of time.

It did develop over a long period of time, but hardly naturally. We have found Dale Spender's book *Man Made Language* (See Appendix C) especially instructive in providing historical background on the use of male generic language. Much that we report in this section is drawn from her work.

It was not until 1553 that Thomas Wilson, writing for an almost exclusively male audience in England, argued that it was more "natural" to place the man before the woman in statements—that is, to say "husband and wife" rather than "wife and husband." Implied in this insistence that males take precedence is the belief that males "come first" in the natural order and are therefore superior. Females of Wilson's time had, of course, no opportunity to protest this so-called natural order. By 1646 Joshua Poole built on this concept to argue that it was not only natural that the male should take "pride of place," it was also proper because, according to him, the male gender was the "worthier" gender.

The concept of male superiority was furthered when in 1746 John Kirkby composed his "Eighty-Eight Grammatical Rules." These rules, dreamed up by Kirkby himself, contained among them Rule #21, which stated that the male gender was "more comprehensive" than the female. This arbitrary rule changed the proposition that males are more important into one that argues that male is the universal category, that male is the norm. This rule gained acceptance among male grammarians and was gradually forced upon others. Women had no voice in the shaping of the rule but were expected to follow it even though it meant the enhancing of the male image and the diminishing of the female.

Finally this principle was encoded in an 1850 Act of Parliament that insisted that "he" legally stood for "she." This concept was then taken up by the educational and publishing establishment, but in spite of vigorous attempts to enforce it, resistance to it continued. For example, people still insisted on using "they" or "their" with a singular indefinite pronoun. They knew instinctively that there was something wrong with grammarians insisting on a rule that did not make sense. Today, after centuries of attempting to stamp out such use by the educational establishment, the National Council of Teachers of English says that it is appropriate to use "they" or "their" with an indefinite singlar pronoun. So instead of saying "Everyone who goes to church should bring *his* Bible," as grammarians taught it, it is appropriate to say "Everyone who goes to church should bring *their* Bible."

No less an authority than the *Oxford English Dictionary* now says that the use of "man" as a generic term is obsolete. We are finally beginning to see the reversal of the damaging rules dreamed up by male grammarians many years ago.

So when people accuse us of "tampering" with the language, we ask, "Just who is doing the tampering?" The truth is that our language has already been tampered with. What we propose is struggling to find ways to remove some of the artificial and unjustifiable rules created by male grammarians many years ago and imposed upon the population as a whole.

Linguists point out that it is crucial to do this work of helping to change the language, because when our language through its rules promotes the use of the symbol *man* at the expense of *woman* it unjustifiably emphasizes the visibility and primacy of males. We are given the message, consciously or unconsciously, that males are worthier, more comprehensive, and superior to females.

A similar study could be made, we believe, of the use of masculine God language in the Christian faith. The Bible contains a much wider variety of images for God—male, female, and nongender—than we usually receive in contemporary writing and preaching. It could well be that the almost exclusive usage of God as "Father" gained ascendency in developments parallel with the secular development of "he"/"man" language.

## Contemporary Psychology and Sociology and Sexist Language

The arguments for the importance of language in our lives and the negative effect of sexist language are now beginning to be verified not only through reason and personal experience but also through studies in contemporary psychology and sociology. For example, the fact that people do not really think generically when they hear or see "he"/"man" language has been shown in a number of studies.

College students were presented with a series of statements containing "man" and "he" in a context that clearly allowed a generic interpretation of these words. Rather than responding inclusively by saying that such terms referred to either or both sexes, the students tended to identify the subjects as males. Males were selected 407 times and females only 53 times. The tendency is overwhelmingly to image male when generic language is used, even when the context would easily allow male and female.[1]

The power of language in affecting our total state of health has been investigated by a medical doctor, W.C. Ellerbroek.[2] Dr. Ellerbroek hypothesized that a major cause of hard-core acne (acne that does not respond to any known medical treatment) was the low self-image such sufferers had as a result of the words they used to think about and describe themselves. Dr. Ellerbroek designed a treatment that consisted only in helping his patients find new words that provoked much more positive images of themselves. The results of his work were dramatic. At least 80 percent of Ellerbroek's patients showed 80 to 94 percent improvement in eight weeks. No other method of treating chronic acne sufferers that has been scientifically studied obtains anything like these results. In fact, a 50-percent rate of clinical improvement and patient satisfaction is considered outstanding.

Ellerbroek's study parallels in many ways the highly unusual treatment for cancer developed by Dr. Carl Simonton and Stephanie Mathews-Simonton.[3] Although their method includes several different treatments related to diet and life style, one of the most important parts of their treatment is visualization therapy. They encourage patients to visualize the cancer being defeated and to see themselves

---

1. See V. Kidd, "A Study of the Images Produced Through the Use of the Male Pronoun As the Generic," *Moments in Contemporary Rhetoric and Communication* 1 (1971):25–29.

2. W. C. Ellerbroek, "Language, Thought and Disease," *Co-Evolution Quarterly* 17 (Spring 1978):30–38.

3. Carl Simonton and Stephanie Mathews-Simonton, *Getting Well Again* (Los Angeles: J. P. Tarcher, 1978).

well again. Their success rates even with persons who have been given up on by traditional medicine are phenomenal.

The work of Dr. Ellerbroek and the Simontons helps to underline what we have already experienced as pastoral counselors and what many other counselors both secular and religious have shared with us. Counselors are finding that low self-image is one of the most persistent problems facing people, especially women, in our society. We believe that sexist language is a direct contributor to this low self-image among women. We believe, too, that such language has a profound impact on our psychological and even physical health, an impact we are only now just beginning to measure. The old adage "Sticks and stones can break my bones but names can never hurt me" was undoubtedly made up to try to handle some of the profound hurt that language can bring. Contrary to the adage, we argue that names (that is, language) do indeed hurt and may even have life and death power over us.

# 3. The Biblical Witness: Stumbling Block or Stepping Stone?

The Bible has often been used to support the status quo and in no area is this more true than in the role and rights of women. This practice runs contrary, however, to the basic message of Jesus, which calls for change—change in the lives of human beings and thus change in the world as a whole. To seek to keep things as they are because that's the way they've always been is contrary to the Gospel message. God is always working for positive change. If we would work with God, we too must seek to transform the world and do away with those attitudes, customs, and theologies that are demeaning and dehumanizing to God's children, female or male.

One of the most common ways in which the Bible has been used against women, and thus misused, is by singling out specific passages that seem to portray women as inferior and holding up this idea as the absolute word of God. This amounts to a veritable worship of the biblical passage rather than of God, herself/himself—a kind of bibliolatry. God's revelation to human beings, including the biblical writers, is always distorted by our humanness, our imperfection, our own sinfulness. To say that every single passage in the Bible is the absolute truth of God is to claim unerring perception of God on the part of human beings, as well as to deify the cultural circumstances in which the revelation was given.

The Bible can be viewed somewhat like the proverbial forest that one can't see for the trees. By treating each and every passage as having value and significance equal to every other one, without ever looking at the main thrusts, the basic themes, one misses the larger meaning of what is said throughout the Bible.

In addition to using the Bible to justify the status quo, people have also used it to put women down. Beginning with the book of Genesis and the creation story, both men and women alike have interpreted the role and status of women to be inferior to that of men. Woman was created last (according to Gen. 2) and therefore she is of lesser importance in the eyes of God, being something of an afterthought. (Undoubtedly if Adam had been created last, he would still have been seen as having greater importance, being considered the very pinnacle of creation. In fact, the argument is often used that the human is greater than the other animals because Adam was created last, after all the rest of creation. If we follow that line of reasoning, should we not carry it out to its logical conclusion and say that woman is superior to man because she was created last?)

If the creation story is understood by Christians to be the theological basis for woman's inferiority to man, what then is to be done with the account of creation given in Genesis 1:26–31? For here woman is not created last but at the same time as man. If the fact of Eve's creation at a later point in time than Adam's and her being created out of Adam (Gen. 2:21–23) is proof positive of women's inferiority, ought not her creation at the same time and from the same source as Adam (Gen. 1:26–31) be proof of her equality with men?

It is not surprising that male church leaders sought to ignore the account in Genesis 1 when referring to the creation story as the theological basis for woman's inferiority. "Let a woman learn in silence with all submissiveness. I permit no woman to teach or to have authority over men; she is to keep silent. *For Adam was formed first, then Eve;* and Adam was not deceived, but the woman was deceived and became a transgressor" (1 Tim. 2:11–14, our italics).

Here Eve's later appearance on earth is tied to The Fall, for which she is given the total blame.

In Paul's first letter to the Corinthians, the second creation story is cited as justification for woman's lesser status. "For a man ought not to cover his head, since he is the image and glory of God; but woman is the glory of man. (For man was not made from woman, but woman from man. Neither was man created for woman, but woman for man)" (1 Cor. 11:7-9). In all of this, the creation story from Genesis 1 is totally ignored. However, it is not in Genesis 2, but only in Genesis 1, where the male and female are created together, that man (humanity) is affirmed to be made in God's image.

It is significant, then, that when Jesus refers to the creation story (in relation to marriage), he refers to the Genesis 1 account, saying, "But *from the beginning* of creation, 'God made them male and female' " (Mark 10:6, our italics). Clearly he understood male and female to have been created equal "from the beginning."

Paul does go on, however, to attempt to counteract what he has just said. "Nevertheless, in the Lord woman is not independent of man nor man of woman: for as woman was made from man, so man is now born of woman. And all things are from God" (1 Cor. 11:11-12).

Why is it that still today in our churches when the creation story is talked about and taught to little children it is almost always the second of the two stories that is told? Many people, including adults, are not even aware that another version of the story appears in the Bible. One can clearly see that the way we use the Bible greatly influences what he hear the Bible saying. If we totally ignore one of the creation stories, rather than holding them both in tension, we are likely to get a distorted message.

Another way the creation story has been used to justify a second-class status for females is by seeing them as helpers or "helpmeets" for males. Because the Hebrew used the word *'ezer* (translated "helper") for Eve, it has been assumed that this means a secondary status subordinate to the more important male. However, such an interpretation merely reflects the sexist bias of the interpreters, for the word 'ezer does not carry the connotation of subordination. It has many uses in the Old Testament and in the majority of cases it refers to God. Certainly God is not subordinate to humans. Psalm 121 is a good example of its application to God. "My help comes from the Lord, who made heaven and earth." 'Ezer describes a certain kind of relationship, a relationship of care and concern between two parties; it does not refer to status within the relationship.

We need also to examine more carefully the words that follow 'ezer in our English translations. The Revised Standard Version of the Bible says a helper "fit for" Adam and the King James Version says a "help meet" for him (not one word, "helpmeet," as sometimes read). What does it mean to be "fit for" or "meet for"? The answer to that question can be found in the story itself. In attempting to make a help fit for the man, God made the animals (Gen. 2:18–20). But the animals were not fit for the man and so God made a woman, equal in every way to the man, a helper fit for him. Phyllis Trible, Old Testament scholar, says it this way: "God is the helper superior to man; the animals are helpers inferior to man; woman is the helper equal to man."[1]

Clearly both the creation stories (Gen. 1 and Gen. 2) witness to the equality and harmony between the male and the female. There is no hierarchy of status when it comes to woman and man. However, in Genesis 3, after The Fall, with the entrance of sin into the garden and into the relationship between human beings, we see this harmony destroyed and the man "lording it over" the woman. In Christ, the "new Adam," this harmony is restored once again.

---

1. Phyllis Trible, "Depatriarchalizing in Biblical Interpretation," *Journal of the Academy of Religion* 41 (1973): 36.

"There is neither Jew nor Greek, there is neither slave nor free, there is neither male nor female; for you are all one in Christ Jesus" (Gal. 3:28).

The passages in the Bible that have caused the most controversy and the most oppression for women are the ones usually attributed to the apostle Paul. Some of these passages undoubtedly were not written by Paul but by others, perhaps disciples of Paul. No matter who wrote them, however, they still have a great deal of power and authority for a large number of people in our churches today. Let's take a look at some of them.

A passage quoted frequently by those who would support the superiority of the male is one to which we have already referred, 1 Timothy 2:11–15: "Let a woman learn in silence with all submissiveness. I permit no woman to teach or to have authority over men; she is to keep silent. For Adam was formed first, then Eve; and Adam was not deceived, but the woman was deceived and became a transgressor. Yet woman will be saved through bearing children, if she continues in faith and love and holiness, with modesty." We not only have the subordination of women held up as part of God's divine plan, stemming from only one of the creation accounts, but we have here a new addition to the Gospel: Woman shall be saved through bearing children—if she also continues in the faith. This theology seems to be quite far removed from that of Jesus, who never once made mention of such a prerequisite for the salvation of women. In fact, when such an understanding was merely hinted at, Jesus quickly corrected it. To the woman in the crowd who shouted, "Blessed is the womb that bore you, and the breasts that you sucked!" Jesus responded, "Blessed rather are those who hear the word of God and keep it!" (Luke 11:27b, 28). Jesus saw no division in the requirements for men and women. Both were to be judged according to the same standards.

Another troublesome passage is found in Ephesians. Here the

writer says, "Be subject to one another out of reverence for Christ. Wives, be subject to your husbands, as to the Lord. For the husband is the head of the wife as Christ is the head of the church, his body, and is himself its Savior. As the church is subject to Christ, so let wives also be subject in everything to their husbands. Husbands, love your wives, as Christ loved the church and gave himself up for her . . ." (Eph. 5:21–26). Most people who use this verse as a model for the Christian marriage forget to read verse 21, which says that the general principal being outlined is that of *mutual* subjection. "Be subject *to one another* [our italics] out of reverence for Christ." They also ignore the meaning of the special injunction to husbands to love their wives "as Christ loved the church and gave himself up for her." The wife subjects herself to her husband because he first subjected himself to her ("We love because he first loved us"). Is not the author entreating the husband to be subject to the wife as much as the wife to the husband? In addition to interpreting the entire passage as one calling for the total domination of husbands over wives, a common error has been to carry the generalization beyond the marriage roles and insist upon the total submission of *all* women to *all* men. Surely that is not the intent of this passage.

A third and similar passage is found in the third chapter of Colossians in which the writer exhorts, "Wives, be subject to your husbands, as is fitting the Lord. Husbands, love your wives, and do not be harsh with them" (Col. 3:18, 19). Here again, the specific situation is the marital one and cannot be applied to the relationship of men and women beyond marriage. What is true for the husband-wife relationship need not be true for all relationships between the sexes. But, further, what we are reading about here is the accepted husband-wife relationship of an extremely patriarchal society that existed 2,000 years ago, not necessarily the God-ordained order of male-female husband-wife relationships for all time.

We must continually remind ourselves that the Bible was written by human beings who were deeply influenced by the culture in which they found themselves, just as we are today. Naturally, the culture affected the way in which they wrote about the revelations of God. It is indeed unfortunate that as we read the Bible we so often confuse the precepts of first-century Palestinian culture with absolute truth.

The Church has also used the Bible to oppress women by making special note that the Bible says Jesus chose only men for his closest disciples. Some denominations have long used this argument to deny women entrance to the ordained ministry or ordained priesthood. Let's look closer at this argument. First of all, it is true that Jesus did not choose any women to be a part of the inner circle of those nearest to him. What is the significance of that fact? It is commonly agreed that the twelve disciples "represented" the Twelve Tribes of Israel. It was also commonly understood that when the Messiah came he would reestablish the Twelve Tribes. Given the status of women in the Jewish religion, and the fact that ritually only males could be true Israelites in the fullest sense of the word, the symbolism of the Twelve Tribes would have been lost in the eyes of the Jewish community had women been included in the twelve. As to women being excluded from ministry because the twelve disciples were all male, it should be noted that the original apostles performed once and for all time the function of representing the Twelve Tribes of Israel. There is no reason to view the ordained minister of today as continuing that function. Women are not asking to be apostles, they are asking to be ministers. Of course, if one really insists that women should not be ordained because Jesus called no women, it should be pointed out that neither did Jesus call any Gentiles. Does that mean that only Jews should be ordained as Christian ministers?

Second, if Jesus had chosen women as a part of the twelve, they would have been subjected to an unnecessary amount of public ridicule by living so intimately with a group of men. In a time when women's relationships to men other than their husbands were minimal, it would have been most difficult for any women involved. Exposing women to that kind of ridicule and loss of reputation was never a part of Jesus' ministry.

However, it should be noted that women were indeed a part of the larger group of disciples that followed Jesus around the countryside. Some of them even helped to support Jesus' ministry financially. Luke reports that Jesus "went on through cities and villages, preaching and bringing the good news of the kingdom of God. And the twelve were with him, and also some women who had been healed of evil spirits and infirmities: Mary, called Magdalene, from whom seven demons had gone out; and Joanna, the wife of Chuza, Herod's steward; and Susanna; and many others, who provided for them out of their means" (Luke 8:1–3). So women were definitely a part of Jesus' public ministry even though they were not a part of the inner circle.

In fact, one of the main thrusts of Jesus' ministry and of the New Testament is the affirmation of the worth of women and their equality with men. Not once is there recorded an incident in Jesus' ministry nor any words of his indicating that women are second to men in any way. To the contrary, his every relationship with women affirmed their dignity as persons equal with men in the sight of God. Of course, in order to do so Jesus had to break severely with the status quo which denied women such worth.

Many of us, reading the Gospels out of a twentieth-century background, are not aware of the tremendous significance of Jesus' actions toward women. For instance, it seems only natural for Jesus to talk with a woman at the well where he stopped for a drink of water. Once we become aware of the fact that rabbis (teachers) in that culture did not ordinarily speak with women in public, Jesus' action takes on new meaning. It was felt that a learned man such as a rabbi was simply wasting his time talking about religious concerns with

women or indeed talking with them at all. Thus, there was a great
deal of prejudice against such conversations between the sexes. This
particular story is often interpreted as indicating Jesus' lack of prejudice against Samaritans, but the remark made by the writer of John
indicates something else at work here. "Just then the disciples came.
They marveled that he was talking with a *woman* . . ." (John 4:27,
our italics). It should also be noted that Jesus was not just passing the
time of day with this woman; he was revealing for the first time that
he was the expected Messiah. "The woman said to him, 'I know that
Messiah is coming (he who is called Christ); when he comes, he will
show us all things.' Jesus said to her, 'I who speak to you am he' "
(John 4:25, 26).

In a similar instance, in the home of his good friends Mary and
Martha, Jesus encouraged a woman to listen and converse with him
about spiritual matters. When Martha complained to Jesus that
Mary wasn't playing the traditional feminine role of preparing and
serving food to the men, Jesus affirmed that Mary was doing the
right thing. "Martha, Martha, you are anxious and troubled about
many things; one thing is needful. Mary has chosen the good por-
tion, which shall not be taken away from her" (Luke 10:38). Unfortunately, the Church has not generally paid much attention to this
passage and has insisted that the "proper" role for women in the
Church is not the intellectual one but rather that of the housekeeper,
thereby denying both women and men the opportunity to choose
how they will use their own unique and God-given talents.

Still another incident from Jesus' ministry bears examination,
namely that a woman (or women) was the first witness to his resurrection. Most Christians are so used to hearing the Easter story that
much of its impact concerning women is lost. While we've grown
accustomed to hearing how Jesus first appeared to Mary Magdalene
after the resurrection, we've missed the real significance of this appearance. To make a woman the first witness to such an extraordi-

nary and significant event was totally unknown in Jesus' time. In fact, in the society of Jesus' day the witness of women was not even acceptable in a court of law. In spite of this, Jesus appeared first of all to a woman. Partly because of the extraordinariness of the event, but partly out of a lack of trust in the words of women, the men refused to believe them: "but these words seemed to them an idle tale, and they did not believe them" (Luke 24:11).

In the new order Jesus is ushering in, women are to be given their rightful status and dignity as daughters of God, equal in every way to the sons of God. If in a fallen, unredeemed state women were seen as inferior to men ("yet your desire shall be for your husband, and he shall rule over you," Gen. 3:16), now that the world has been redeemed through Jesus Christ, woman is to be restored to her rightful place as equal to man.

Nowhere is woman's status in this new order made more clear than in Paul's dramatic reversal of the old prayer of thanksgiving prayed daily by the Jewish males. Paul, being a devout Jew, no doubt prayed with his fellow Jews, "Praised be God that he has not created me a Gentile; praised be God that he has not created me a woman; praised be God that he has not created me an ignorant man" (or a slave). When Paul became a Christian, however, he said, "There is neither Jew nor Greek, there is neither slave nor free, there is neither male nor female; for you are all one in Christ Jesus (Gal. 3:28). In Christ there is a new order of creation.

At various times in history the truth of Paul's statement has been seriously questioned, but out of the controversies came a greater appreciation and affirmation of the truth it embodies. In the first century, one of the arguments revolved around the line "There is neither Jew nor Greek." There were those who insisted that in order to be "in Christ" one must first become a Jew by submitting to circumcision. The essence of this position was to contend that there was indeed both Jew and Greek and that being a Jew was in some sense better than being a Greek, since Jewishness was a prerequisite for becoming a Christian. In the nineteenth century the second line of that passage was severely tested by the Church as it struggled with the question of slavery, finally deciding that human slavery was inconsistent with the Christian faith. Now, in the twentieth century, it is our turn to struggle with the final line in that trilogy: "There is neither male nor female." What does that statement mean in relation to sexist worship? What does it say about the stereotyping of roles within the Church? About decision making at all levels of the Church? About the witness the Church makes to society in regard to women? About the seriousness or lack of seriousness with which the Church takes the liberation of women?

Is the Bible a stumbling block to women's liberation? We think not. It is our conviction that the overwhelming witness of the Bible, and the New Testament in particular, is a witness for the full personhood of all people, including women. Specifically, this also means a clear call for the elimination of sexist attitudes and traditions within the worship service. Worship, as it is usually conducted in most Christian churches today, is sexist and goes against the teachings of Jesus. If we would follow Christ in treating women as whole persons, significant in the eyes of God, we must begin today to affirm the worth of women within the context of worship.

# 4. Freeing Our Concept of God from Sexism

God as Mother. "Impossible!" you say. "Blasphemy!" Didn't Jesus himself call God "Father"? What makes us so reluctant to think of God in feminine terms? Have masculinity and divinity become so bound up with each other that it is blasphemous to think of God as feminine?

Perhaps it would be helpful in dealing with this question to look first at why Jesus might have addressed God as "Father" and asked us to do the same. Jesus was trying to express that God loves all human beings, regardless of wealth, position, or status. One of the best metaphors to use in getting this idea across is the metaphor of the father who loves his children and not merely tolerates them. In a patriarchal society such as the one in which Jesus lived, what better image could he use to indicate God's care and concern? By calling God "Father" Jesus was also saying that God is accessible; we should communicate with God in much the same way we communicate with another human being, such as our earthly father. The accessibility of God was especially highlighted by Jesus through the Aramaic word he chose for God. The word *Abba* is really best translated "Daddy." It was the early cry of the infant in its parent's arms and may have been directed to both father and mother.

Finally, Jesus was saying that God is due the same kind of respect that children in a patriarchal society gave their father. None of these ideas is betrayed today, however, by calling God "Mother."

And Jesus himself did not deny the feminine within God. Quite the contrary. In telling the parable of the lost coin (Luke 15:8–10), Jesus cast a woman in the role of the God who searches and searches until the one lost coin (human being) is found. A simple story, perhaps, but one with profound ramifications. But most of us are so accustomed to thinking of God as a male that we don't even make the connection between God and the woman in this parable.

Let's go back now to the statement that calling God "he" doesn't mean we actually think of God as a male. How many times have you heard someone talk about God as "the *man* upstairs?" Why is it that when children are asked to describe God they almost always describe a *man*, usually complete with long white beard? Artists too have contributed to this idea. (Michelangelo is a notorious example of one who used this kind of imagery; witness the Sistine Chapel.) Clearly, the mental picture of God that most of us get is one of a male being, and this mental picture profoundly influences our concept of God.

If "he," "him," and "his" when applied to God actually do not designate *maleness*, but rather are used "generically"—that is, to mean that God includes both male and female—then there should be no objection to using "she," "her," and "hers" in reference to God also. The fact that people do get upset, or perhaps more frequently laugh, in the rare instances when God is called "she," indicates that our conception of God as strictly male is much more deeply entrenched than we will admit.

For all of their patriarchal ways, even the Jewish writers of the Old Testament did not always use masculine imagery to describe God. In Deuteronomy 32:18 (RSV) we find the words, "You were unmindful of the Rock that begot (or bore) you, and you forgot the God who gave you birth." Here is a passage that definitely pictures God as feminine. And again in Isaiah 42:14: "For a long time I have held my peace, I have kept still and restrained myself; now I will cry out like a woman in travail, I will gasp and pant." What do we do with these passages? For too long the answer has been, "Ignore them." The time has come to take them seriously as we struggle to know

God more fully. We need to hear these passages just as distinctly as those that speak of God's masculinity. Granted, there are not so many of these passages, but the fact that these words were sounded at all in a patriarchal religion and society is cause to take them seriously today.

But maybe you are thinking, "Why all the fuss? Can't we leave the time-tested concepts of God alone and just try to serve him (*sic*)?" There are at least two reasons why the answer to that question must be a resounding "No!"

First of all, an ever increasing number of women are discovering that they feel a basic alienation from the masculine God of traditional Christianity at the very point of their sexuality. How can they, female human beings, identify themselves with a masculine God? When a woman tries to pattern herself after the highest and best that she knows, she discovers a deep schism that cuts her off from her God, a God who is totally other than she. Not only is there the basic difference between the Creator and the creature that all humans experience, but there is also the difference between male and female. This sense of otherness does not exist as completely for most males, for when they look to God they experience a oneness with God at the point of their masculinity. In striving to be like Christ, they share with him not only the human experience but the masculine experience as well. For a woman there is no such shared sexuality.

Second, and even more important, there is the firm conviction of growing numbers of women that God is trying to reveal another aspect of "himself" to us today. In the past we have recognized the masculine aspects of God. Now it is time to recognize God's feminine aspects as well. If God is revealing himself/herself to us, we must be willing to open our minds and hearts to that revelation.

It is noteworthy that while we have clung tenaciously to a masculine "Father" God in the Christian church, we have nevertheless found subtle ways of attempting to incorporate the feminine within that masculine God. One of the most common of these attempts is to say "Mother Nature" when speaking of God's creative activity in the world. "*Mother Nature* dressed the trees in gorgeous autumn colors" means the same thing to many as saying that "God dressed the trees in gorgeous autumn colors." Somehow we can accept Mother Nature, but Mother God—that's another story!

God is often described as compassionate, kind, gentle, forgiving, loving, tender—qualities that have traditionally been assigned to the female sex rather than the male sex in our culture. The irony comes when we take these so-called feminine qualities and apply them to God. The God who possesses the "feminine" characteristics is then labeled "Father." We can picture God as being like our culture's ideal mother, but we refuse to admit what we are doing and we refuse consciously to see God as being in any way feminine. Is femininity so inferior to masculinity that we feel we would be showing God disrespect to apply to God the feminine labels such as "Mother" or "Queen?"

The Roman Catholic Church has dealt with this need to recognize God's femininity and masculinity by elevating Mary's role as Virgin Mother to a position of divinity or near divinity. While this role has often been ridiculed by Protestants, it may be that such a theology comes nearer the truth than does the Protestant theology with its heavy masculine bias. It is interesting that today, when women are gaining in status and the idea of God as totally masculine is being challenged, Mary's prominence is declining. This is as it should be, for the need to divinize Mary disappears when God's own femininity is acknowledged and affirmed.

The masculinity of God has certainly been supported by the Incarnation in Jesus Christ, a male. We in no way deny the masculinity of Jesus, but we do deny the great significance that has been attached to it by the Church. All of us are familiar with pictures of the Nativity showing a Chinese holy family with a Chinese Christ child, an Indian family with an Indian Christ, a Spanish family, and so on. We do not get angry and upset and say, "That's not the way it was!" Instead, we affirm that Christ's Jewishness did not completely define him, that in a sense he belongs to all races, to all nationalities. Today in Africa and America there is an increasing emphasis on a black Christ. We know, of course, that Jesus was not black, but we can affirm that Christ belongs to the black race as much as to the white, the yellow, the brown, and the red.

Just as Christ was actually a Jew while here physically on earth, so he was also a male. We have recognized that Christ might have been born into any race, and indeed was born into every race in the deepest sense. Just as we have acknowledged that his Jewishness did not totally define Christ, can we not also acknowledge that neither is he totally defined by his maleness? As Christ "belongs" to all races and nationalities, can he not also "belong" to both sexes? We do not often speak of Jesus the *Jew*, but how often we talk about the *man* Jesus! It is as though Christ cannot be separated from his maleness, but he can easily be separated from his Jewishness. There are many people who somehow accept the idea of a black Christ but not a female Christ. But are not Christ's skin color and his sex both of the same essence—incidental to his Christ-ness? If the society had been reversed and Palestine had been a matriarchy instead of a patriarchy, surely God would have sent her Daughter.

We are not saying that there should now be a dramatic switch in our concept of God and that, whereas God in the past was considered masculine, from now on God shall be known as feminine. Not at all. To do that would be to gain absolutely nothing. What we are saying is that it is necessary that we perceive God as containing both the masculine and the feminine, as these qualities have traditionally been understood in our culture. And it is important to realize also that unlike maleness and femaleness, what is "masculine" and what is "feminine" is determined and defined not by nature but by our culture. Of course, God transcends maleness and femaleness since these are human categories. But as long as we have only human experiences and human terms with which to describe God, we will necessarily find ourselves applying human characteristics to God.

For nearly a century the Christian Scientists have spoken of God as both Father and Mother. The time has come for the Church as a whole to reexamine its theology of God and to become aware of the narrow-sightedness with which we have looked upon God. How can we truly call God "Father" if we cannot in the same breath say "Mother?"

While we may express our concept of the masculinity and femininity of God by saying Mother/Father, some find it desirable today to de-emphasize both the parent figure within God and the "sexuality" of God by using terms other than "Mother/Father," "he/she." One problem that people encounter in thinking of God as Mother or Father or Parent is that their understanding of God is greatly influenced by their relationship with their own parents. A person who has not known a loving and trustworthy parent may find it impossible to trust a God whom she or he is encouraged to think of as Father or Mother.

That person may want to think of God as Creator or as Redeemer, titles that imply no gender. Thus, "Father, Son, and Holy Spirit" might become "Creator, Redeemer, and Sustainer" or "Creator, Savior, and Holy Spirit" or any number of other such titles that in no way imply that God is a sexual being. One value of this approach is that it might help us to understand more clearly that God is Spirit and minimize our tendency to anthropomorphize God as "the man upstairs." As we come to affirm that God is Spirit, with qualities that we humans have sometimes understood as either masculine or feminine, we will be better able to worship God in spirit and in truth.

In his book *Is the Bible Sexist?*[1] Donald G. Bloesch states that "the debate over sexist language is ultimately a debate concerning

---

1. Donald G. Bloesch, *Is the Bible Sexist?* (Westchester, IL.: Crossway Books, 1982).

the nature of God." We believe he is right in this statement although wrong in most of his other contentions in the book. The ultimate significance of language is finally tested in our descriptions of God. But rather than following Bloesch and bemoaning the fact that inclusive attempts to describe God lead us to new understandings of God often along the lines of those being developed by process theologians and philosophers, we celebrate this fact. We believe the biblical understanding of God is basically open-ended and that it allows for new developments through history. There is a humility and awe in much that the Bible writers say about God. Developing new images of God, as we do when we are serious about inclusive language, plays into this respect for mystery and provides new insights and experiences. It helps us to realize how hazy our picture of God really has been.

We have found that expanding our images of God in both private and public worship has had a profound influence on our own theological development. We have experimented with taking a different image for God each week for our own personal meditations. One week we would pray to "Light," another week to "Rock," another to "Father," another to "Mother," and so on. There are well over a hundred different images for God found in the Bible alone. To unearth some of these treasures and appropriate them in our own spiritual life is a real adventure.

One definition of heresy is that it is "part of the truth parading as the whole." When we use only the image of "God the Father" in public worship we are guilty of heresy just as surely as if we were denying the divinity of Jesus. We owe it to our congregations to make use of the many marvelous images for God. This is one way of saying to ourselves and our congregations that we do not have God in a box, that God is always "the beyond in our midst"—always more than any of our images can fully capture.

# 5. Sexism in Hymns

The problem of sexist hymns seems more difficult than some other sexist language problems in worship. If your church mimeographs its bulletins, the pastor and/or worship committee have control over the language of prayers, litanies, sermon titles, and so forth, but you usually have invested considerable money in the hymnals you use each Sunday. As these books are already there, and filled with sexism, what can you do about them?

There are four approaches you can use to deal with the problem of a sexist hymnal. First, there are many hymns in all the major denominational hymnals that are not sexist. You should analyze your hymnal and make a list of these hymns for your use (also see Appendix A).

Second, many of the sexist hymns in the hymnal can be changed (edited) to make them inclusive in language. The new words to the hymn can be reproduced in the bulletin or flashed on a screen by means of an overhead or slide projector. If this alternative is selected with copyrighted material, however, you must be sure to obtain permission to reproduce either the words or music or both from the copyright owner. If you do not, you are opening yourself to suit by the copyright holder.

Third, encourage interested persons in your congregation to write new hymns either to old hymn tunes or folk tunes or to their own original music. When you encourage this creativity, also help the persons involved to see how important it is to avoid sexism in their creations.

The fourth alternative is an excellent one for many congregations—the purchasing of an alternative companion hymnal to use along with the regular hymnal. There are now several inclusive langauge hymnals available, any one of which would make an excellent supplement to a regular denominational hymnal.

In this chapter we would like to examine each of these alternatives in detail, spending a majority of our energies on number four.

Choosing nonsexist hymns from the hymnal your congregation uses regularly can be a good first step. However, a quick analysis of these hymns from almost any of the denominational hymnals quickly shows that they lack much in variety and often in quality. Many of the hymns that meet inclusive language guidelines come from the nineteenth-century evangelistic period with its heavy emphasis on a personal relationship with Jesus. This is not the place to debate the merits of that style of theology, but it is certainly true that a church that relies too heavily on hymns of that period is depriving itself of the many other great theological emphases down through history. Certainly most congregations will have to use additional alternatives to choosing only those hymns in their present hymnal that are nonsexist.

Editing hymns to make them more inclusive is the second alternative. Purists immediately raise a question about the ethical implications of changing an author's work. This is an important question that needs response.

A study of the history of hymnody quickly shows that churches have not been afraid to change hymns down through history for various reasons: to make them more meaningful, to shorten them, or to make them more contemporary. Even a comparison of the same hymn in several different hymnals will show how many changes the text of a hymn has undergone. Often different verses and different words within a verse are found in these hymnals. On the one hand, a person could raise objection to this practice and ask, "What right does the church have to tamper with an individual poet's creation?"

On the other hand, there is merit in the observation that when
something like a hymn is composed for the liturgy of the church, it
becomes a gift to the church as a whole, a gift the church, if it wishes,
may alter to make it a more effective part of the liturgy. In this sense,
a hymn is seen to be a kind of folk song—a song of the people, to be
expanded, contracted, and changed over a period of many years.
Whether or not one feels such change in hymnody is right, it is a fact
that it has occurred throughout history. Sometimes the changes may
not even have been for the best—for example, the inclusive "Faith of
the Martyrs" was changed to "Faith of Our Fathers." Another way
to envision this concept is to argue that we need to restore to hymnody the notion of an oral tradition, a continually evolving mode of
story telling, address, and description.

So hymns that have a long history within the Church (seventy-five
years or more) may have already had a number of changes in their
texts. To change them further may be seen as part of the natural
process of creating pieces that speak more adequately to a particular
time and place in history. If such changes are made, however, they
must be done with sensitivity and care. Nothing angers some members of a congregation more than to have an old favorite hymn
changed from the way they have known it. Such change can be a
consciousness raiser, but if it occurs without adequate preparation it
may result in more negative than positive reaction.

Sometimes it is also quite difficult to find appropriate inclusive
substitutes. When you are dealing with hymnody you are working
not only with the meaning of words but also with syllables, rhythms,
and sometimes even rhyme. Sometimes it can be almost impossible
to find an inclusive word that really fits a hymn. Often rather than
make an awkward and obvious editorial change, you should recast a whole line or even a whole stanza. Some useful inclusive equiv-
alents include "folk" for "men," "one" for "man," "parent" or
"Mother/Father" for "Father," "familyhood" for "brotherhood,"

"neighbor" or "other" for "brother," "humans" or "people" for "mankind."

In hymnody and liturgy the Church is often referred to as "she," as are inanimate objects in common speech. People will often apply the feminine pronoun "she" or "her" to things such as cars, ships, planes, and so on. Many women find it demeaning to be classed in the same category as "things," realizing that the masculine pronouns "he," "him," and "his" are reserved for human beings alone. When speaking of a genderless object such as a car or a genderless institution such as the Church, it is appropriate, and for many women essential, to use the neuter pronoun "it" rather than the feminine "she."

Many people have asked us about the word "Amen." "Is that not a sexist term?" they wonder. Actually no, since "Amen" is a Hebrew word meaning "So be it" and has nothing whatever to do with men. However, you might find it more meaningful occasionally to substitute "So be it" for "Amen" at the conclusion of hymns and prayers. "Alleluia" or "Hallelujah," meaning "Praise God" in Greek and Hebrew respectively, might also be substituted. And, of course, the current phrase "All Right" will speak to some people more clearly than "Amen."

Copyright laws add a new wrinkle to discussion about changing hymns. We believe the concept of a hymn being part of the oral tradition of the Church is still a good one with contemporary music, but copyright laws restrict this changing process. If a hymn is copyrighted it should not be changed without permission from the copyright holder. Many contemporary hymn writers have said that they want their earlier compositions changed to be inclusive in language. These include such persons as Avery and Marsh and the St. Louis Jesuits. The St. Louis Jesuits have even produced a pamphlet listing all the changes to inclusive language they want people to make in their earlier compositions. Many other composers, when approached, are glad to give their blessings to such changes. It is a difficult and time-consuming job, however, to track down and then write or call the copyright holders of hymns you wish to use each week in worship. For this reason, groups that choose to edit hymns to make them more inclusive are often limited to older hymns in the common domain and the few newer ones they have time to get special permission to change. Of course, they need special permission to reproduce any copyrighted hymn in any form with or without changes, and sometimes fees charged by companies or individuals to do this are exorbitant. This means that yet other alternatives usually need to be investigated.

One of the best ways to accomplish the third suggestion for obtaining nonsexist hymns—that of having persons in your congregation write new, original hymns—is to have periodic hymn-composing workshops. Whoever leads such sessions should be sure that the persons involved clearly know what sexism in hymns is and why it is so damaging. Perhaps sections of Chapters 1 and 2 from this book can be discussed with them so they begin to understand what such sexism does to an increasing number of women. These workshops do not necessarily need to be large—two or three persons who have a gift in this area can be tremendously valuable in providing many fresh hymns for your congregation.

This brings us to the fourth alternative—supplying an inclusive language hymnal to your congregation to be used along with its older hymnal. Many congregations have already done this. Many others have provided other hymnals or songbooks that are contemporary in style but not inclusive in language. Because a number of good inclusive resources now exist, we believe such an action holds great promise for providing a congregation with a large number of inclusive language hymns for regular use in worship. We would like to look at three of these resources in depth and mention briefly several others. All three of these hymnals take sexist language concerns with utmost seriousness. They provide resources that are inclusive not only in their language for the people of God, but also in their language about God. You do not find in them any generic references to people as "men," "sons," or "brothers." You also do not find references to God as "Father," "Lord," "King," or even "He," unless they are balanced with words like "Mother," "Queen," or "She." (Information for obtaining the hymnals mentioned is provided in Appendix C.)

We waited for several years for someone to produce a nonsexist hymnal and when no one did we edited our own. *Sisters and Brothers, Sing!* contains over 135 nonsexist hymns and has proved extremely popular with a wide variety of groups from senior high and college groups to women's organizations, to entire congregations. It also contains an extensive section of worship resources such as calls to worship, prayers of confession, acts of dedication, and so on. It is the only inclusive language hymnal that we know of to include these kinds of resources in addition to hymns.

*Sisters and Brothers, Sing!* contains hymns that are already nonsexist. It is not a rewriting or paraphrasing of hymns to make them inclusive, although it does contain one or two familiar hymn tunes with new words. The book contains a wide variety of styles of music although it is weighted toward folk type songs. It includes some traditional hymns such as "Amazing Grace" and many contemporary folk hymns by some of the great writers of today, including Joe Wise, Barbara Neighbors Deal, and Carey Landrey. It contains melodic line and guitar chords for all songs and piano accompaniment for some. The songs are divided into sections according to basic elements in worship services: praise and prayer, confession and assurance, affirmation, communion, dedication, and benediction. Also included are a number of songs especially for children as well as songs and worship resources for special seasons such as Christmas and Easter.

Both of the other hymnals we want to discuss are newer and include a large number of rewritten hymns—new inclusive words to old familiar hymns. We were resistant to this approach for several years because we felt it called undue attention to the language issue, often before a congregation had been adequately prepared for it. We also felt that the rewrites were often awkward and weak when compared to the original hymns. However, the two hymnals we are about to discuss have helped to change our minds on this. Both of them provide quality transformations of old hymns, and we believe that both of them have made a real contribution to the struggle for inclusive hymnody.

*Everflowing Streams,* edited by Ruth C. Duck and Michael G. Bausch, is a blend of new hymns and rewrites of old ones. The quality of the rewrites is quite good. It includes piano accompaniment for almost all the 83 hymns and several songs by co-editor Ruth C. Duck, who is a most gifted contemporary hymn writer. Although it does not contain worship resources, its companion volume, *Bread for the Journey,* edited by Ruth C. Duck, does provide such resources organized around the Christian year. It, too, is a valuable resource.

*A New Hymnal* by Steve Rose takes seriously the concerns of sexism, classism, racism, and militarism; it is mostly a rewrite of older hymns (83) but also contains some new ones (17). Steve Rose is a wonderfully gifted poet and song writer and his own songs are a tremendous plus to the volume. His rewrites of older hymns are revelations to read because he says so much so gracefully through his changes; we see them less as "rewrites" than as transformations into new and exciting hymns for today. He categorizes his changes by placing from one to three asterisks by the hymns to indicate minor to major changes. This hymnal includes only melodic line for the hymns and does not contain additional worship resources.

It is fascinating to take a well-known hymn such as "The Church's One Foundation" and sing it first in the version we usually find in denominational hymnals and then in the version found in *Everflowing*

*Streams* and then in the version found in *A New Hymnal.* The changes are different and significant in both new versions. Singing these different words has quite an impact on a group and is a good way to get into a discussion on the impact of words in a hymn.

A number of other new hymnals or songbooks in addition to the three already mentioned are also available. *Because We Are One People,* published by the Ecumenical Women's Center in Chicago, is a shorter attempt to rewrite old hymns. It was the first published resource that we know of to rewrite hymns and, in our opinion, the two books already mentioned do a better job.

The United Methodist Church's Section on Worship has issued a new *Supplement to the Book of Hymns.* Although it does fairly well in its language for people, it does fairly poorly in its language for God. Still, it has some excellent songs in it.

*Seeds of Hope* is a most helpful meditation and worship/music resource, described by its creator, Art Allen, as "a collection of songs with supporting thoughts and illustrations." The songs are organized under such topics as "Growing," "Drought," "Stump, Sprout," and "Feasting." Included are more than fifty songs, all written by Art Allen, touching many of the concerns of contemporary worship, an easy-to-use reprint license form (enabling congregations to use these songs legally in worship by reimbursing him a modest 2¢ per copy), and helpful topical and scripture indexes.

A small hymnal entitled *Gather to Remember,* edited by Michael A. Cymbala, has much of the finest writing by contemporary Roman Catholic musicians. Unfortunately, it, too, is not generally sensitive to concerns about language for God. The same is true for another fine new Roman Catholic hymnal, *Life Songs.*

Hymns are powerful instruments of our faith. When all else about a service is forgotten we may still be humming or singing lines from one of the hymns. Because of their sustaining power, it is especially important that we work to eliminate sexism in our hymns.

# 6. Liberating the Liturgy

There are two major aspects of the liturgy that need to be liberated—its language and its leadership.

All that we said concerning changing language in our chapter on hymns applies here, too, except that it is often not so necessary to match up syllable, rhyme, and rhythm. Therefore, it is usually not difficult to take each part of your liturgical language and edit out the sexism. In addition to editing old prayers and responses, you should be open to the tremendous possibilities of using new prayers and responses. Examples of such contemporary elements of liturgy are presented in the next chapter. We hope they are enough to get you started. The more persons in your congregation that you can get to help write new prayers and responses, the more your liturgy will truly become the work of the people. Many churches now have liturgy committees that meet weekly to develop the worship service for the coming Sunday. Membership on these committees is rotated so that many persons in a congregation have an opportunity to experience helping to create a worship service.

One question often asked when we talk about liberating the language of worship is "What about sexist language found in the Bible—do we have the right to edit that?" Some people feel that any "tampering" with the Bible is anathema and reject out of hand any possibility for editing out sexist language. They forget that the Bibles they are using are themselves translations of early manuscripts which do not always agree.[1] But even if we had the original manu-

---

1. For an interesting treatment of the way male translators of the biblical texts have shown their male bias, see the article by Ruth Hoppin listed in Appendix C.

scripts of the Old and New Testaments and an agreed upon, or literal, translation, undoubtedly there would continue to be much sexist language in the Bible. After all, it does reflect the highly patriarchal climate in which it was written.

Some persons feel we should leave this language as is, recognizing that the Bible was written in a particular historical period and is bound to reflect some of the culture and language of that period. These persons point out that the amazing thing about the New Testament is not that it contains some sexist language, but that it so often and so clearly sees women in a new equality with men. They also point out that if we justify editing out the sexism in our Bibles, some other group will want to edit out something else, and pretty soon some of the eternal validity of the Bible will be erased by groups who have modernized it on this issue and that.

Such an argument appears wise at first blush. Certainly we must be careful not to change the Bible. A study of Church history quickly teaches us that what one generation doesn't understand or finds objectionable in the Bible, other generations find meaningful. If we begin editing the Bible to meet our own tastes, we will weaken its power to confront us with words we may not wish to hear.

But to eliminate the sexist language of the Bible is, as we see it, much more in the realm of a contemporary translation or amplification, such as the work of J. B. Phillips, than it is changing the Bible. The job of a translator is to try to put the words and meanings of the original writers in contemporary and understandable language. For instance, where the words "man"[2] or "sons" are used generically, they ought to be translated for our contemporary society into words that convey their full meaning, such as "human" or "sons and daughters." This is not changing the real meaning of the words or

---

2. The word generally translated "man" in English is actually the Greek word for "human being."

even editing out large sections of the Bible but is instead amplifying the meaning of the original words.

Our problem is that as of now no version of the Bible has done this. The one that we have found often coming the closest is The New English Bible. Even this translation, however, has much needless sexist language. What we, the authors, are doing until a non-sexist version of the Bible is produced is simply inserting the appropriate changes as we read. We do this in our imaginations as we read passages for our own study and meditation, and we do it also as we read the Scripture in worship. We encourage others who read Scripture during worship to do the same, stating as they do so that they are reading a paraphrase of Scripture.

Liberating the leadership in worship services may prove to be an even more difficult task than freeing its language. Because the overwhelming majority of ministers are men, liturgy leadership is already dangerously overbalanced. Protestant seminaries all over the country, however, are reporting record enrollments of women in their programs for ordination, so this overbalance may correct itself, at least partially, in a few years. Until then, it will be doubly important to have lay persons involved in the leadership of worship, and in most cases these lay persons should be women, to balance the male clergy.

Many churches already have lay persons assist with the worship services. If your church does not do this, you will want to help it begin this practice. Such leadership makes sense theologically—worship is a congregation's theology acted out and certainly lay representatives of the congregation should be involved in the leadership of this experience. Unfortunately, even those churches that have used lay leadership have most often used men rather than women. This is especially true of large prestigious churches.

How do you go about balancing the liturgical leadership in your own church? If you are the pastor of a local church, you can simply choose persons of the opposite sex to help you lead the liturgy. It's certainly permissible to choose two women and a man to help you in some services, only one woman in others. The important thing is that balance in leadership be maintained. If you are a lay person, you will have to try to convince your pastor that this balance is important. Some of the discussions in Chapters 1 and 2 of this book might be helpful here. Make sure your pastor realizes that the majority of persons attending churches across the country are women, and that they are often totally left out of the worship leadership. When you have talked with your pastor, don't be satisfied with an occasional token woman as worship leader. If your pastor is male, ask him how he would feel if most of the persons in the congregation were male but only occasionally did a male ever participate in worship leadership.

One of the problems you may face as you attempt to effect a balance of worship leadership is the response from many women that they don't want to be leaders because they get frightened before a group. This comes from men, too, but not so often. This is a very real fear, and it should not be treated lightly. Often it comes out of deep feelings of inferiority that have been pressed upon women for many years. Because of these feelings some women may not want to lead in worship services. We must respect their feelings at this point and not attempt to pressure them into something they don't wish to do. Other women can be found who will want to provide such leadership. What may help women want to lead in worship is to provide a training course for worship leaders. At one church we served, all lay worship leaders where required to take a special six-week training course. This dealt with theology and worship, but it also dealt with practical matters such as speaking before a group, using a microphone, reading Scripture with meaning, and so forth. We found this to be one of our most fruitful adult education experiences. We also found that it gave new confidence to persons who were fearful when standing before an audience. In addition, we found that as women become accustomed to seeing other women leading worship, they often gain confidence in their own ability to be worship leaders.

Another possible problem in extending liturgical leadership to women is the condescending attitude often conveyed by male ministers. Such phrases as "the lovely ladies" or "What would our church do without its wonderful women's societies?" often betray a view of women as almost children, to be cajoled, patted on the head, tolerated in a benign way. It is extremely important that such an attitude be confronted and changed. The most perfectly balanced liturgical leadership with the best nonsexist language in hymns, prayers, and responses can still be torpedoed by such an attitude. Again the only way we know to handle this is through education and sometimes through gentle but firm pressure. As it is often unconscious behavior, so the first step then may be helping the pastor become aware of what he is doing.

When we speak of liberating the liturgy, we must also see the possibilities for bringing greater variety in dress and tone. Women involved in leading worship should not have to wear the black scholar's robe that many male ministers still wear. They should be encouraged to use their imaginations to come up with new and more appropriate liturgical garb. If they do this, the men who lead in worship, both clerical and lay, may see new possibilities for their own liturgical dress. We have found liturgical ponchos quite effective, for example. They can be made out of homespun or cotton and then liturgical symbols for the various seasons of the church year, or for particular services, can be embroidered or sewn on. We usually use a white material on which various colored symbols are sewn. All different colors of liturgical garb are appropriate, however, and if worship leaders begin using more colors, this may help lift the drabness from many services.

Not only is it important to make sure that sexism is eliminated from both the language of the liturgy and from its leadership, it is also essential that even small details connected with the service reflect the equality of the sexes. Perhaps this is nowhere more true than in the listing of names in the worship bulletin. For many years in most organizations it has been customary to list married women in relation to their husbands. Thus, listings of officers in the women's society of a church often read Mrs. Harold Jones, president; Mrs. John Rider, vice-president, and so on. This manner of listing names only serves to perpetuate the myth that women gain their identity and their importance through men. It implies that a married woman is simply an appendage of her husband. It has often been said that "in marriage the two become one and that one is the husband." The most blatant example of that kind of fallacious thinking is shown by referring to a husband and wife as "the Steven Johnsons."

Further, the traditional titles of Miss and Mrs. seem to be saying that for a woman the most important identifying characteristic is whether or not she is attached to a man by means of marriage. In common practice titles are often used with women's names while they are not with men's names. Names in a bulletin thus appear as follows: James Olsen, Mrs. Philip Carter, Miss Grace Thompson, Richard Henderson, and so on. One can only assume that the reason the titles are necessary for women but unnecessary for men is to indicate the woman's relationship or lack of relationship to a man.

Perhaps the best way to deal with this problem is simply to eliminate the use of titles. In the Church, where we claim to be "brothers and sisters in Christ," why should we address each other as "Mr." or "Mrs."? Would it not be better to use our "Christian names" in addressing one another, as we do the brothers and sisters in our own families?

If titles must be used, the corresponding title to "Mr." should be "Ms." and not "Mrs." or "Miss." If a woman insists on being called Mrs., with her husband's name, that is her right, but such designation should certainly not be encouraged.

Some women object to the title "Ms." because they do not want

to risk disapproval by society and by males, in particular, by identifying themselves in any way with the women's liberation movement.
Others prefer to be called Mrs., with their husbands' names, simply
because that has been the custom in which they grew up. They will
say that "Ms." is all right for younger women but not for themselves.
However, the issue at stake here is not what custom one feels comfortable with, but whether naming and identifying women in relation to men is demeaning to women. More and more women are
deciding that it definitely is demeaning and that such a custom
denies the full personhood of women.

Although this book focuses on spoken, written, and sung language
in worship, we want to point out the fact that much of our communication is given and received nonverbally. Communication theorists
estimate that 7 percent of what we say is received by the words we
speak and 93 percent by our tone of voice, gestures, posture, and so on.
This means major attention needs to be paid to our nonverbal style if
we are concerned about effective communication.

It is in the area of the nonverbal that women clergy can play an
especially important role. Their very presence in the pulpit and at the
communion table is itself a tremendously powerful statement on the
equality of the sexes, but women also have gifts in communication
from which all persons may benefit.

Rather than imitate men's speech patterns and gestures (usually
low voices and angular movements), women clergy can capitalize on
their higher voices and their more flowing, circular gestures. (While
there is some evidence that these patterns, including pitch of voice,
are culturally conditioned, they are, nevertheless, a reality in most
instances.) Preaching may have fallen into some disrepute because
for a long while it was too much dominated by the intense, masculine, rationalistic debate model. With the advent of increasing numbers of women in the pulpit we are finding even the male clergy
adopting new varieties of dress (the alb especially) and different

styles of preaching (much more emphasis on story telling, for example).

Women can bring a new artfulness and gentleness to preaching. They can also help congregations remove preachers from the pedestal. Generally women are not automatically granted the same authority as men, and so are not so likely to be the objects of a false kind of authority and power—stand-ins for God. Instead, they have to earn respect and authority by their words and actions, not by their office. Thus by their presence in pulpits, women help to bring greater truth and realism to the way in which all pastors, male and female, are viewed by congregations.

Women ministers are also helping congregations to see that worship should not be a spectator sport. Several female and a couple of male ministers we know who have had training in dance are helping congregations as a whole use their bodies more effectively and beautifully through simple gestures to songs and prayers and through processionals and dances. This is really a recovery of lost practices in worship, as is pointed out in detail by Michael E. Moynahan in the tape series entitled *Embodied Prayer*.[3]

Liberating the liturgy is not an easy task. People often resist tenaciously any changes in what they consider to be treasured ritual. Many pastors become accustomed to a particular style of leadership and are not eager to change it. Do not become discouraged. Be willing to go slowly and accomplish your victory piecemeal. But do not give up or be fooled into thinking that no movement is slow movement. Change can and will come. The last chapter of this book gives some more detailed strategy that may be helpful to you when you find persons both in leadership and in the congregation resisting such change.

---

3. Michael E. Moynahan, *Embodied Prayer*, National Catholic Reporter, A-1200.

# 7. Liberated Prayers, Affirmations, and Responses

The editing suggestions made in Chapters 5 and 6 should also help you in rewriting prayers and responses, both traditional and contemporary, but you may feel a special need for more contemporary nonsexist liturgical expressions. There has been an abundance of contemporary worship resources produced in the last several years. Unfortunately, still far too few are totally nonsexist. In fact, many of the so-called modern worship resources are more sexist than some older liturgical expressions. This is true because many modern liturgies stress our social responsibilities and our relationship to one another (with words such as "brother" and "mankind" used in abundance), whereas older liturgies tended to emphasize one's personal relationship to God. Therefore, we offer you a beginning selection of truly contemporary resources. These are intended to be only examples of what can be done. We hope you'll take them as such and develop your own creative liturgical resources from them.

You will note that in many of the prayers and responses we simply repeat the word "God" whenever it is used rather than attempt a pronoun such as "he/she" or rather than use a new term such as "parent." We feel that at the beginning of change in worship the use of "God" repeated when necessary rather than some new way of speaking of God will be less jarring to persons who are worshipping. As education concerning the concept of God progresses, it will be natural to refer to God with combined pronouns and with words such as "parent."

In this chapter we divide the resources according to the basic parts of most worship services. (We realize that not all worship services use all the categories we show and that others undoubtedly have additional ones.) You will discover too as you read through this section that some of what is written can be adapted to other portions of your worship service. Don't hesitate to take what you feel is most meaningful to you and adapt it to be more useful to you.

The prayers and responses in this chapter are original with us in one sense, but dependent upon many others in another sense. As far as we know, we have originated or contributed to the particular wording in all these liturgical resources, but we realize that we have been affected by thousands of worship services we have experienced over many years. Often there are phrases and prayers in these services that have remained with us and become a part of who we both are. Usually, no credit is given on bulletins as to where a particular prayer or response has been obtained. In a sense we feel this is good because it helps to show the anonymous creative community throughout Christendom that is sharing without thought of personal credit what to them has been a most meaningful and significant response to God. We are sure we have been influenced more than we know by this great creative community. So if you read a phrase or paragraph that sounds much like something you have seen elsewhere, you probably *have* seen it somewhere else. This is our proclamation of thanks to all those creative persons who have helped us as we try to develop the most meaningful liturgical resources possible.

One further comment is important here. We think that most contemporary worship resources are far too wordy. Because words in worship are so important, we believe they should be used with economy. We feel that in many contemporary services so great an attempt has been made to include every idea that nothing is said well enough to be remembered. Words are fragile and delicate instruments and when they are piled up on top of each other, especially in things that congregations are to read together, they tend to become meaningless and boring. Some of the most meaningful services we have experienced have been completely nonverbal communion services. Our society is beginning again also to recognize the tremendous value of silence, the universal language. So as you develop your own liturgical responses, remember to hold your words reverently and use them sparingly.

## Calls to Worship

LEADER: In the beginning there was the energy of creation . . . and it moved. And God said—"Light!"

CONGREGATION: *And there is light. And the energy continued to move . . . and God said, "Space!"*

LEADER: And there *is* space. And the energy continued to move . . . and God said, "Earth!"

CONGREGATION: *And there is earth. And the energy kept moving . . and God said, "Male and Female!"*

LEADER: And there *is* male and female . . . and we are here. And now the earth is ours to inherit, and the gifts of the earth.

CONGREGATION: *And so we come to worship to celebrate these gifts and to learn again what it means to be entrusted with them.*

\*      \*      \*

LEADER: Why are we gathered at this time and place?

CONGREGATION: *We are gathered as the people of God—to hold before us the mirror of the world, and the mirror that is Jesus Christ our Savior, and with these mirrors to see ourselves as we are and should be.*

LEADER: Then let us together praise the Christ—before whom we eternally stand.

\*      \*      \*

LEADER: Welcome in the name of the One who was no stranger to sorrow and who knew death so that we might more fully know life.

CONGREGATION: *We are children of God. We stand in communion with all persons everywhere. We come to this place today to hear again of God's fantastic love that calls us to a transforming care that literally reaches 'round the world.*

\*          \*          \*

LEADER: Good morning!

CONGREGATION: *Good morning!*

LEADER: Let us come together in the spirit of the One who unites us all;

CONGREGATION: *In the spirit of our Savior, Jesus Christ.*

LEADER: Let us remember that we are God's chosen people;

CONGREGATION: *Chosen to be God's servants in the world.*

LEADER: We gather because of our common need for renewal.

CONGREGATION: *Let us offer acceptable worship to God who renews us for service. Amen.*

\*          \*          \*

LEADER: We come together to thank the Creator of life.

CONGREGATION: *We come to praise God's holy name and to seek after God's ways.*

LEADER: We come to be forgiven and to forgive.

CONGREGATION: *We come to be a community in God's love.*

LEADER: We come, in short, to worship.

CONGREGATION: *Praise God.*

\*          \*          \*

LEADER: "I am the door. Come in. Do not be afraid." This is what Jesus says to those who stand half-secure behind half-shut doors.

CONGREGATION: *This is Jesus' saying to all the children of the earth who cling to their blankets of sin like silent crutches.*

LEADER: There are those moments when in the name of Jesus bold and certain people on earth must say: "Come in. Do not be afraid. It is I."

CONGREGATION: *Christ waits. There is room for all to come in, even through the half-open door. Sister and brother, come now. Come and learn and live.*

*   *   *

LEADER: Now is the time to live: to come to the God who creates us, to sing to the Redeemer who frees us.

CONGREGATION: *Now is the time to come alive, to invite the whole world to join in praising God.*

LEADER: Yes, now is the time to invite the sky to thunder God's word, the earth to rumble in praise.

CONGREGATION: *We invite all to celebrate with us, to glorify God's name, to dance with God's Spirit, which fills us.*

*   *   *

LEADER: To worship is to heighten our awareness of the poetry of our existence.

CONGREGATION: *It is to open all the windows of our being to the indwelling power of God's love.*

LEADER: It is to join the mighty chorus of praise and thanksgiving that has boomed out since the beginning of creation.

CONGREGATION: *To worship is joy. It's great to be here!*

*   *   *

LEADER: "Behold, I stand at the door and knock. . . ."

CONGREGATION: *And what is that supposed to mean?*

LEADER: It's a way of saying that God is always seeking us.

CONGREGATION: *But has God found us?*

LEADER: God only fully finds us when we want to open ourselves to God's love. God does not force us; we must respond.

CONGREGATION: *The first step, then, is from God, and the response is our responsibility?*

LEADER: Right! And that's what worship is all about. Through worship we open doors through which the Spirit of God may move, and we can respond.

\*          \*          \*

LEADER: Why did you come here this morning?

CONGREGATION: *To find God.*

LEADER: I didn't know God was lost.

CONGREGATION: *God is lost so often in the busy routine of our daily lives. We come here today to open our lives to the invasion of God's life.*

LEADER: Well, let's get busy!

\*          \*          \*

LEADER: In an age of computer magic when all the volumes of history are literally at our fingertips,

CONGREGATION: *We dare to come to worship a God who was once a tiny, helpless baby.*

LEADER: In an age of self-discovery when people spend a fortune to find their "real" selves,

CONGREGATION: *We dare to come to worship a God who believed in losing life to find it.*

LEADER: In an age of comfort when many indulge themselves with the latest conveniences in perfect heating, lighting, and dining,

CONGREGATION: *We dare to come to worship a God who had no place to call home and who wandered with the poor and outcast.*

LEADER: In an age when we have everything, what more could we possibly want?

CONGREGATION: *We come to worship today to hear of the One who knew what life and loving are all about. We come to find a reason for our living and motivation for our love. We come to be changed by the God who lived and died and was raised for us. We come because, although we may seem to have everything, we often lack the one thing that is needful—love.*

\*        \*        \*

LEADER: Hear the sound; it is in the air.

CONGREGATION: *What sound? We don't hear anything.*

LEADER: You can't hear it? Listen carefully.

CONGREGATION: *Nothing.*

LEADER: We come to worship to uncover the sound of God at work in the world. It is in the common, the ordinary. We may find it in the loving word a wife utters to her husband, the care a youngster shows to a disappointed friend, the cooing of a baby happy with the world.

CONGREGATION: *We come to worship to sharpen our hearing. Let us hear God's presence in new ways today.*

\*        \*        \*

LEADER: We come together today to learn about reverence.

CONGREGATION: *We worship because we know that Christ was a living example of reverence.*

LEADER: Help us to remember the tenderness and love Jesus showed as he walked this earth.

CONGREGATION: *And help us in this service to see how Christ can help us live more reverently in our daily lives.*

\*        \*        \*

LEADER: We live under a razor's edge of death. At any moment the big bombs could begin dropping.

CONGREGATION: *And so we are here today out of desperation. In the midst of all our daily dangers, we come to find peace in Christ and new energy to become peacemakers in our world while there is still time.*

\*        \*        \*

## Invocations and Collects

### *Invocations*

God, you're here, waiting for us. Before we ever thought of trying to find you, you came out to meet us. We're entering a treasured ritual now. It may be out of habit. It may be that someone forced us to come here. It may be that we are hungry or wistful. For whatever reason, we are here. Capture our minds and hearts and wills, so that we may worship you honestly and meet you truly. In the Spirit of Christ. So be it.

\*        \*        \*

God, may the presence of your Holy Spirit, which is everywhere, be especially here now comforting us but also confronting us with the responsibility to make your word of love become flesh in our actions today. Amen.

\*        \*        \*

Amazing God, may the presence of your Holy Spirit descend upon your Church once more, awakening us and filling us with love and joy and power till Christ's love is alive in every human heart. Amen.

\*        \*        \*

LEADER: Come, Holy Spirit!
CONGREGATION: *Inspire us in this hour of worship.*
LEADER: Inspire us so that we can breathe new life into old dreams.
CONGREGATION: *So that we can lose ourselves to find ourselves.*

LEADER: So that we can love without counting the cost.
CONGREGATION: *Come, Holy Spirit!*

\*       \*       \*

God, it almost seems presumptuous for us to ask you to be here with us. We know you're here already. But we also know that often we don't bother to be aware of your presence. Make us aware now in this time we've set aside for special sensitivity to you. Help us to be open to you and through you to others. Amen.

\*       \*       \*

God, may the presence of your Holy Spirit bring us alive inside to the wonder of love that reveals you everywhere. Amen.

\*       \*       \*

LEADER: God, we know that your Spirit hovers over us like a big bird.
CONGREGATION: *Help us to see your bright wings.*
LEADER: Help us to hear the cooing of your love in our own lives and all over the world.
CONGREGATION: *Help us to feel the warmth of your presence.*
LEADER: Help us to be the winged presence of your love to each other.
CONGREGATION: *Now and forever. Alleluia!*

\*       \*       \*

God, you're here waiting for us. Help us in this hour to wait for you. In our waiting help us to discover that life is never all it should be or can be and that expectation is essential to discovering new possibilities for your presence in us. Amen.

\*       \*       \*

LEADER (raising hands): Alleluia!
CONGREGATION (raising hands): *Alleluia!*

LEADER (reaching out to put hands around the shoulders of persons nearby): God is here.

CONGREGATION (reaching out to put hands around the shoulders of persons nearby): *God is here.*

LEADER (raising hands): Alleluia!

CONGREGATION (raising hands): *Alleluia!*

LEADER (crossing hands in front of body): Have no fear.

CONGREGATION (crossing hands in front of body): *Have no fear.*

LEADER: We thank you, Holy Spirit, that you are with us, giving encouragement in the midst of our problems and pains. We affirm your presence at the beginning of this service. May we be open to its courageous power today. Amen.

*       *       *

Come, Holy Spirit, inspire us with your grace. Bring us comfort and love in the midst of our fearful times. Help us to know your presence powerfully in this worship time today. Amen.

*       *       *

LEADER: Don't forget the Spirit.

CONGREGATION: *What?*

LEADER: Don't forget the Spirit. It is so easy to do, to worship without Spirit, to plod through a service only half alive.

CONGREGATION: *You mean we should be enthusiastic?*

LEADER: Yes. We should be alive with energy and excitement because the very Spirit that hovered over the world at creation and was with Jesus at the baptism and brooded over the world at Hiroshima is with us today. And it has bright wings.

CONGREGATION: *Bright wings?*

LEADER: Bright wings to transform our ordinary living into something with excitement and power and courage. The wings of God's love are with us today.

CONGREGATION: *Alight on us this hour and enlighten us with your holy love. Amen.*

*       *       *

LEADER: "Spirit of the living God, fall afresh on me."

CONGREGATION: *Fall?*

LEADER: It's an old hymn. It's a way of asking God to be especially present with us in this worship service.

CONGREGATION: *Fall?*

LEADER: Well, can you say it better?

CONGREGATION: *Spirit of God, dwell in us today. Pervade us like the blood of our bodies, filling us with your love and joy and peace. Amen.*

*       *       *

## Collects

God, who comes to us in our great joys, our crushing sorrows, and in all the everydayness in between, be with us now as we share ourselves with one another in this time of worship. In Jesus' name we pray. Amen.

*       *       *

Amazing God, whose glory outshines the sun, open our lives to the inspiration of your Holy Spirit that we may more fully reflect the glory of your love. In Christ's name we pray. Amen.

*       *       *

God, who split the veil of the Holy of Holies when Jesus was raised, rip the veils from our hearts this day so that we may come alive to your love for us and for all persons. Alleluia!

*       *       *

God, whose love is revealed in the tenderness of a mother's smile, help us to reflect the miracle of your tenderness and gentleness in our lives today. In Jesus' name we pray. Amen.

\*          \*          \*

God, who brought light from darkness, help us to see your light so well that it not only illumines our path but reflects off us to illumine others. We pray this prayer in the name of the One who was called the Light of the World. Amen.

\*          \*          \*

God, who gave us the miracle of music, help us to bring our lives in tune with your will so well that true harmony can reign on earth. In Christ's name we pray. Amen.

\*          \*          \*

God, who in the person of Jesus died out on evil rather than striking back at it, help us to see the futility of force and violence as principles for our own lives or for our nation. We pray this prayer in the name of the One who gave his life for peace. Amen.

\*          \*          \*

God, who burst open Jesus' tomb, break open the tombs of indifference and despair that trap our lives. In Christ's name we pray. Amen.

\*          \*          \*

God, whose arms reach around all the griefs of the ages, be with us today and help us with the particular griefs that invade each of our lives. In Jesus' name we pray. Amen.

\*          \*          \*

God—who loves all people as a mother loves her children, not because they are good but simply because they are—show us the way to

love all your children as our sisters and brothers, simply because they
are human. Amen.

*     *     *

O God, in whom we were conceived and given birth, give us now the
rocklike strength to stand firm in our commitment to you when
others chase after false gods. Amen.

*     *     *

God, whose capacity goes beyond all our greatest computers, help us
to make sense out of the universe you have given us, whether it be
studied in the tiniest atom or in the most expansive charts of the
universe. Enable us to see your design, your wisdom, in all of creation. Amen.

*     *     *

O Divine Light, show us more clearly your radiance in those around
us. Help us to treat one another with the reverence you have for each of
us. In Christ's name we pray. Amen.

*     *     *

Mother God, help us to get used to calling you by this name. It is in so
naming you that we can begin to see you more fully in graceful and
tender ways. And such naming will also mean that we can see women
more divinely. For such vision we pray. Amen.

*     *     *

Father God, let us hear this name with new understanding. May we
see how calling you "Father" transforms our vision of fathers and
gives us a closeness to you that we need desperately—the closeness of
ideal parental love, be it from father or mother. Help us to call you
both Father and Mother and in that calling transform our notions of
both. Amen.

\*          \*          \*

O God, who is like an everflowing stream, flow into us today. We need your healing, cooling waters. We are tired and thirsty for the love you can supply. Flow like a river in us today. Amen.

\*          \*          \*

O God, who is the liberator of us all, remind us today of the captives. Make us actively concerned about those in prison or imprisoned by circumstances beyond their control. Sensitize us to the ways we are each captive to particular desires and problems. Liberate us and our world beginning today! Amen.

\*          \*          \*

O Divine Judge, look on us today not with your justice but with your mercy; or help us to see how your justice and mercy are really blended in your love. May we not fear your judgment because we know your love. In Christ's name we pray.

\*          \*          \*

Be our vision today, O God, so that we may see with new eyes. Show us the sparks of your renewing love in the most hopeless people and situations we know. Let us look upon our world today with the eyes of faith, knowing that finally everything is upheld in your perfect love. Amen.

\*          \*          \*

O God, whose steadfastness outdoes the sun, help us in this worship service to lean on your steady love. May we feel the strength of your care for us in the midst of all our heartaches. In Christ's name we pray. Amen.

\*          \*          \*

## Confession

### *Calls to Confession*

There is something wrong in us and around us. Let us admit it.

*     *     *

Christ is a mirror revealing to us how far we have fallen short of God's perfect love. We must admit our failures before God, for this is the only way we can receive new strength to live more effectively.

*     *     *

We know better than we do. Let us confess the failures of our love and the confusion of our lives.

*     *     *

Let us confess honestly before God the things that we have done or failed to do that have caused us to be less effective servants.

*     *     *

We would like to look at ourselves and be wholly pleased with what we see. But the Christian Gospel calls us to be honest. It forces us to be realistic. Let us, then, make a bold recognition that we are not pleased with what we see.

*     *     *

[Read selected headlines from today's newspaper showing evil, ugliness, and pain in the world.] We have heard of some of our world's pain and heartbreak. Let us admit our involvement in it.

*     *     *

Sin is missing the mark of our high calling to love like Jesus. Let us admit some of the ways we have missed this mark.

*     *     *

When we let envy, greed, resentment, lust, and selfishness eat away in us, we can be destroyed. I call you now with me to admit our wrongs before God, knowing that such confession is essential to the health of our souls.

*     *     *

There is much hurt and sadness in our world and in us. Let us lay some of this heartbreak before God as we admit that we help to cause it.

*     *     *

I ask you now to join me in an act of courage as we confess our sins, as we invite the searchlight of God's love to probe into the darkest places of ourselves and our world.

*     *     *

As Christians we are called to speak out clearly and pay up personally for the injustices of our world. But before we can do this with integrity, we must confess our own implications in these injustices. Join me in this confession.

*     *     *

### General Prayers of Confession
*(Prayed by all)*

O God, we admit that too often we live on the surface of life. We are afraid of the depths, though we try to hide many things deep within us. We are haunted by the knowledge that we have hurt others by our own selfish acts. We are harassed by the realization that our sense of priorities and laziness have prevented us from responding to situations where me might have made a creative difference. What gets into us, God, to make us miss the mark of our Christian love time after time? Help us, O God, we pray. Amen.

\*     \*     \*

LEADER: Let us confess our sin and admit who we are.

Left: *We are impatient and bored.*

Right: *We are often undisciplined and irresponsible.*

COMMUNITY: *Yes, Jesus; that's the way it is.*

Left: *We care about the poor and the oppressed.*

Right: *And we also care about cool buildings, comfortable chairs, color TV, and three good meals a day.*

COMMUNITY: *Yes, Jesus; that's the way it is.*

Left: *We are not sensitive enough to others.*

Right: *And too sensitive to ourselves.*

COMMUNITY: *Yes, Jesus; that's the way it is.*

\*     \*     \*

God, we come before you knowing we have tried to hide from you, from one another, and from ourselves. Somehow we have felt that by depending upon our own powers we could solve the problems of life. We have tried to escape by withdrawing from the difficult, the challenging, the crucifying experiences of life. We have become trapped in a meaningless round of insignificant activities while we have avoided projects we should have done. We have strayed far from the fullness of life you have promised us. Forgive us for our self-centeredness, our proudness, our weakness, our blindness. Have mercy upon us, that we may become your people anew. So be it.

\*     \*     \*

God, we confess that we are frightened and humbled by the violence and hatred that we see rampant in our society and feel sometimes in ourselves. Forgive us for our lack of understanding and love. Help us to bear up under hatred and persecution and courageously stand for peace and justice. In Christ's name we pray. Amen.

\*          \*          \*

O God, we admit that too often we see our lives as a burden to be borne rather than as a joy to be celebrated. Forgive us for getting bogged down in all our problems and heartaches. Help us to realize the joyous miracle of your love, even in the midst of discouragement and despair. In Christ's name we pray. Amen.

\*          \*          \*

God, we turn to you to get the inside track and obtain special favors. We ask for your direction in our lives only when it coincides with the direction we want to go. We want your power only when it will help us with our own pet projects. We ask for your sanction for our ambitions. We want you to give us a blank check that we can fill out however we wish. Help us listen for what is your will for our lives. Help us be open to being used by you rather than trying to use you. In Christ's name we pray. Amen.

\*          \*          \*

Mother and Father God, we know how often our world is torn by hatred and misunderstanding, and we know how much this pains you. We know that we are not personally responsible for all of this tornness, but we also know we stand guilty for some of it. There have been times when we have been quick to accuse and slow to forgive. There have been times when we have let small differences mushroom into vast difficulties while at the same time we have ignored important understandings that should have drawn us together in love. For our tendency to push hate before love and angry accusation before patient understanding, forgive us God. In Christ's name we pray. Amen.

\*       \*       \*

God, forgive us for being asleep so often when you need us. You
writhe in the agony of the world's hunger while we worry over
whether to have steak or chicken tonight. You weep with the soul of
a person who is friendless while we fret over whom to invite to some
social occasion. Wake us up to the needs of our brothers and sisters
everywhere. In Christ's name we pray. Amen.

\*       \*       \*

I'm sorry for the times someone wasn't beautiful
   and I looked away.
I'm sorry for the times someone stretched out a hand
   and I pretended not to notice.
I'm sorry for the times someone needed to be held
   and I clung to safety instead.
I'm sorry for the times truth was on my tongue
   and I swallowed it instead of speaking it.
I'm sorry for the times love was in my heart
   and I was too embarrassed to express it.
I'm sorry for the times fear was in my heart
   and I didn't trust you with it.
I'm sorry for the times I claimed to be an innocent bystander
   and still I knew that by being a passive participant I was
   guilty for allowing wrong to be done.
I'm sorry for the times strangers asked me for something
   and I pretended not to realize what they needed.
I'm sorry for the times I haven't loved enough
   and the times I haven't loved with all of me.
I know you know I'm sorry, God,
   and I know you've already forgiven me.
Maybe that's why I'm not ashamed to say I'm sorry.

* * *

Father and Mother God, we confess that often we do not like the bodies we have. Sometimes we long for different families. We would exchange our jobs for the jobs of others. We would like to do away with parts of our history. We are afraid of our moods and feelings. We wish we had more time. We would like to start over again. We lust after the prestige of others. We think more money will solve our problems. We resent the injustices we have suffered and cherish our sorrows. We want to be appreciated for our small graces. We are enchanted by the past and enticed by the future. We have never really been understood. In short, we have refused to live because we have held out for better terms. Heal us, God, from the distance we have tried to put between ourselves and life. Restore to us a love for you and for all your creation. Help us be renewed in our whole lives through Jesus Christ our Savior. Amen.

* * *

O Caring One, we come before you as people who do not care enough. We mean well, but so much gets in the way of our doing much about the heartbreaks of our world. The things that trap us and sap the life out of us are often trivial—a better business balance sheet, favorite TV shows, sales on things we don't need, the arcades, sports events. These and a hundred other activities crowd into our lives, making it impossible to find the time or the energy to show real loving care. Forgive us, O God. Amen.

* * *

God, what gets into us? We say we want to be your loving creatures, but we act as if only our own selfish pleasures mattered. We say that we want to worship you, but we act as if such worship is a boring duty to be gotten over as quickly as possible. We say that we want to get involved in causes that will make a positive difference in the world, but we act as if we are always too busy to commit ourselves in any really costly way to these causes. God, our actions are so often different from our intentions. Help us to follow through with the courage and energy to act positively on those matters we know are important for ourselves and our world. Amen.

*       *       *

We admit it, O God, *we are responsible*.
And look what we have created . . .
   a world teetering on the brink of nuclear annihilation.
   millions starving in the midst of pockets of unbelievable plenty.
   a nation posturing in pride while supporting military dictator-
     ships that think nothing of mass bloodshed.
   individuals—you and me—who seem more concerned about to-
     morrow's weather than about today's casualties in war, starva-
     tion, drunken driving, drug abuse, and on and on.
We admit *we are responsible* . . .
   for our own involvements in the concerns we have placed before
     you and that we have added to their power through our actions
     and our inaction.
Shake us awake to the pain of your world, O God.
Help us to take our responsibility more seriously. Amen.

*       *       *

For some of my laughter and tears, O God, forgive me.
   For my laughter when
     it was at the expense of another,
     it was a cover-up to avoid risky conversation.
       Forgive me, O God.
   For my tears when
     they were an escape from involving myself in costly action,

they were a cheap release from problems that deserved more
struggle.

Forgive me, O God.

Let me celebrate both laughter and tears

But only as they help me hold our glorious world gently, tenderly,
lovingly in the depths of my heart. Amen.

\*       \*       \*

### Words of Assurance

LEADER: There is no sin so terrible that God's love cannot forgive. In
the name of Jesus Christ your sins are forgiven.

CONGREGATION: *There is no sin so terrible that God's love cannot forgive. In the name of Jesus Christ your sins are forgiven.*

\*       \*       \*

"The mercy of God is everlasting." Such is the witness of our heri-
tage, which, being interpreted for our times, means: now and in
every moment our every past is accepted, our future is opened, our
every present is offered to us afresh. This is the truth that sets us free.

\*       \*       \*

It's so hard to believe
That it must be said over and over:
"You're O.K., I'm O.K."
God accepts us and loves us just as we are.

\*       \*       \*

The future is open.
Arise, pick up your life, and walk!

\*       \*       \*

One fact remains unchanging—God has loved you, is loving you, and will always love you. That's the good news that brings us new life.

*       *       *

LEADER: Listen! Here is good news: Jesus said, "I will never turn away anyone who comes to me" (John 6:37b, TEV). He has come to forgive you in your failure.
WOMEN: *To accept you as you are,*
MEN: *To set you free,*
ALL: *And to make you what you were meant to be.*

*       *       *

Yes, Jesus—that's the way it is, all right. We can't deny it. We are every name we've called ourselves and some we are afraid to call ourselves. And yet we know that because of your love all our failure is accepted and we are free to live. Hallelujah!

*       *       *

God is never far from any of us (Ps. 125:2). We rejoice in this truth that takes the edge of strangeness off life. No matter where we are or what we do, God is with us, still loving us. That's the most fantastic fact of the universe.

*       *       *

LEADER: Jesus said, "Neither do I condemn you; go and do not sin again (John 8:11b). Our life is given back to us with hope.
CONGREGATION: *Every day is an opportunity to decide again that this day shall not be like the others.*
LEADER: That a new person is being created at this moment, free from the past, with the future open.

CONGREGATION: *We have been freed to live fully in the present; that's the good news of the Gospel.*

*   *   *

God's love is the one constant in our universe. It is to the rock of this love that we can anchor our lives, knowing that "in all things we are more than conquerors through Christ who loves us" beyond all time and space (Rom. 8:37).

*   *   *

LEADER: God says, "There is nothing you can do to make me stop loving you."

CONGREGATION: *When the truth of those words breaks through, we are transformed.*

LEADER: You are accepted and loved as you are. You don't have to carry around the burdens of the past.

CONGREGATION: *We are a new creation through the powerful presence of God's constant love.*

*   *   *

God is like a mother comforting her child in her arms. Stand up, put your arms around yourself, and rock back and forth as a mother rocks her child. As you rock, feel the healing comfort of God's presence with you, knowing that you are God's little girl or God's little boy and that God loves you no matter what.

*   *   *

When you are down and need a friend, Christ is present with you. Christ is a rainbow pointing to the riches of God's love that are there for you in spite of all you have done. Let the rainbow fill your life with the colors of God's caring. Amen.

*     *     *

LEADER: We only appreciate the miracle of a sunrise when we have
waited in darkness.
CONGREGATION: *We have just confessed some of the darkness of our*
*lives.*
LEADER: And now the sunrise—God loves you no matter what.
CONGREGATION: *Daybreak. Alleluia!*

*     *     *

"Forgiveness is the fragrance the violet sheds on the heel that crushes
it." Take now the vial of violet perfume and anoint your neighbor with
the words, "In the name of Christ, you are forgiven." (After the
anointing, during which music may be played, say these words:)
"Breathe deeply. Smell the sweet fragrance of God's forgiveness. May
it cling to you as a constant reminder of God's steadfast love."

*     *     *

Jesus Christ died for our sins not to satisfy an angry God but to reach a
stubborn and selfish people. We are those people. Let the power of
these words sink into you and be comforted: Jesus Christ died for you.
Amen.

*     *     *

## Affirmations of Faith

We believe that God was in love with the world and could not keep
the secret.

The telling of it was CREATION.

We believe that God's love is constantly being shown as creation
continues and continues and continues every moment of every day.

We believe that Jesus is our window to divinity and our mirror of humanity. Through Jesus we find God's love for us fully revealed and we discover that God's will for us is that we love one another in full humanness.

We find God's presence of love with us in the Holy Spirit which often speaks to us in the voices of other people. Therefore we affirm that openness to God and openness to other humans are two sides of the same coin and that really listening to others can help us to hear God.

We believe that God never gives up on us and that nothing can separate us from God's love.

Alleluia. Amen.

\*       \*       \*

LEADER: Let us affirm together why we worship, for in saying this we will also be affirming our faith.

CONGREGATION: *We worship to reveal ourselves to God and to each other, to look for what we have lost, to glue together broken pieces of life, to refit the scattered jigsaw puzzles of our lives and the world's life, to renew our vision of the life of Jesus Christ, that we might know more sharply and unmistakably what Christ's way really means, to seek to get the point of the greatest drama on earth, to find our own roles and learn our own lines from the director of all history.*

\*       \*       \*

I believe in the living God,
   the Parent of all humankind,
   who creates and sustains the universe
   in power and in love.
I believe in Jesus Christ,
   God incarnate on Earth,
   who showed us by his
   words and work,

suffering with others,
and conquest of death,
what human life ought to be
and what God is like.
I believe that the Spirit of God
is present with us now and always,
and can be experienced
in prayer, in forgiveness
in the Word, the Sacraments,
the community of the Church,
and in all that we do. Amen.

\*     \*     \*

We believe that God never gives up on us.
We believe that Jesus was God in human form
who showed us the astounding steadfastness
of God's love for us.
We believe God's Holy Spirit
is always with us
even in times of deep suffering and sorrow.
We know that God's love for us
continues
and continues
and continues.
Nothing.
not even death,
can separate us from this love.

*Alleluia!*

\*     \*     \*

We believe in the One who gives us life as Creator and affirm that we
are called to be witnesses to this creator God in the world. Therefore,

there is no choice for us but to immerse ourselves in the stream of history, accepting our particular place in time and doing the best we can with what we have. We believe that failure to accept responsibility, refusal to take a stand on vital issues, timid rejection of the ties of true belonging are denials of life and of God's will for our lives—they are in fact deeds of death.

We know that the God of all life calls us to affirm life, not become dead to it through timidity and fear. God calls us to do our best to understand the times in which we live, to add our weight to the scales on the side of justice and equality within valid differences. We know that if we live our lives responsibly we need not worry about physical death. Our job is to live out God's love as we have learned it from Jesus right here, right now. God will take care of the rest. *So be it!*

\*          \*          \*

LEADER: Let us recall our faith as God's people.
CONGREGATION: *We believe that God—Creator, Redeemer, and Life Giver—summons the Church to mission in the world:*

*—To witness by word and deed to God's revelation in Christ and the acts of love by which God reconciles us.*

*—To evoke in us the personal response of repentance and faith through which we can find newness of life in loving relationships with God and with our brothers and sisters everywhere.*

*—To bring us together into a Christian community of worship and love, and to send us forth into the world as servants in the struggle for meaning and justice.*

*—To move us to live in awareness of the life-giving power of God's presence, in acknowledgment of God's rule over history, and in the confident expectation of the final completion of God's purpose. Amen.*

\*          \*          \*

LEADER: We are the people of God.

CONGREGATION: *Our lives are eternally significant.*

LEADER: We are the people of the resurrection.

CONGREGATION: *We are free to live to life, and not to death.*

LEADER: We are the people of the covenant.

CONGREGATION: *We live our lives in commitment.*

LEADER: We are a people of *koinonia.*

CONGREGATION: *We live in mutual love and support.*

LEADER: We are the sons and daughters of God.

CONGREGATION: *We live as a family with all boys and girls, men and women everywhere.*

\*     \*     \*

I believe in the love of God revealed in Jesus Christ.

I believe that behind the clouds of life shines the love of God.

I believe that God has a purpose for the world and a purpose for me.

I believe that God wills the blessedness of all lives and of every single life.

I believe that Jesus Christ saves life from the power of sin and sorrow and death.

I believe in the life-giving power and grace of the Holy Spirit.

I believe that through faith and prayer and sacrament I can live the life that is life indeed.

I believe that God calls me to love and service.

I believe that through Christ life leads at last to the fullness of goodness, truth, and beauty.

I believe in the grace of Jesus Christ and the love of God and the communion of the Holy Spirit.

\*     \*     \*

We believe that God is still creating and that we are called to join in this creation.

We believe that God loves us not because Christ died for us, but that Christ died for us because God loves us. And Christ continues to die for us today.

We believe that God's Holy Spirit of love still sets people free and that God calls us to help in this task of liberation.

We believe that "the Church" is a chosen people, not chosen for its own sake, but to be servants of God for the sake of the world.

We believe that God's love is something that will never give up on us, and so we approach the future with confidence.

\*        \*        \*

We believe that God is "all for" us.

We believe that God wants the best for us.

We admit that we often thwart God's desires.

We affirm that our history is filled with God's attempts to break through to us and help us back onto the right track of love and care.

We recognize God's loving presence with us as our ancestors searched for their promised land.

We acknowledge God's care shining through the personal stories of Ruth, Hosea, and Jeremiah.

We celebrate God's full revelation in the miracle of Jesus Christ.

We pledge to take our salvation history seriously as we continue our journey through life.

May God help us be on the track of love and care. Amen.

\*        \*        \*

LEADER: It is an act of uncommon courage to make public affirmation of faith. For some such an act may mean their lives. For us it is only words in worship. But if we begin to hear and live out these words, it will mean our lives too. Let us dare to affirm our faith.

CONGREGATION: *We believe in a continually creating God who calls us to costly love that goes beyond seventy times seven and even the infinity of modern computers.*

*We believe in a continually healing Holy Spirit who calls us always to open our lives to the renewing power of love.*

*We believe in the continually caring community called the Church which is the physical presence of Christ in our world.*

*We believe in a continually growing relationship between ourselves and God which is not ended even by death.*

*   *   *

LEADER: As Christians let us affirm who Christ is for our lives.

CONGREGATION: *Christ was a human being like us. And yet Christ is also different from us.*

*Christ came singing love.*

*Our song is too often fear and hate.*

*Christ lived singing love.*

*Our lives are too often quiet desperations.*

*Christ died singing love.*

*Our deaths are too often raging anger at being cheated by life.*

*Christ rose still singing love.*

*May Christ's spirit rise in us so that we may continue the singing. Amen.*

*   *   *

## The Offering

### *Offertory Prayers*

O Giver of Life, behind this offering lies the busy world of our working: the office, the production line, the home, the classroom, the laboratory. Save us from creating a world where wealth accumulates and people decay. Accept this offering and our lives, limited as they may be, as willing instruments for good in your world. Amen.

*       *       *

We bring you what we have, God: our good intentions, our mixed motives, our limited grasp of truth, our halfhearted commitment, our tiny gifts. None of them, we know, is good enough, but we offer them anyway. And we dare to affirm that they are received. In Jesus' name. Amen.

*       *       *

Mother God, who loves us, in this act we present ourselves: our work and our leisure, our joys and our sorrows, our thoughts and our deeds—just as we are, to be used by you in the world. We humbly ask you to accept our offering as the personal giving of ourselves for the increase of good and in the service of truth, here, and all over the earth. Amen.

*       *       *

God, as we offer our money to you, help us also to be able to offer you ourselves. Take our bodies, our minds, and our spirits and use them for your ministry in your world. Through Jesus Christ. Amen.

*       *       *

God, we know that your gifts cannot be hoarded, that they are for spending. Help us in this time of offering to share with you not only our money but our lives also. How do we need to spend ourselves today? Amen.

*       *       *

God, before the gifts you have given us our gifts pale into insignificance. We are almost ashamed to bring these gifts, because they cost us so little. And yet we know that, just as you accept us though we be unworthy, you accept our gifts. Increase our vision and enlarge our

compassion, that we might embrace all the world's needs as those
that demand a response from us, so that in this world there *shall* be
celebration. Amen.

*     *     *

Clothe the naked and you clothe Jesus—that's what you said, God.
Help us to hear those words—really hear them so that we can begin
to discover that the distance to Heaven is measured by nakedness,
hunger, thirst. Help us to hear these words so well that we begin to
give accordingly. Amen.

*     *     *

Mother/Father, help us to realize that silver and gold are not God,
whether in the form of a golden calf or a bargain counter. Help us to
give ourselves fully to you today as we share our money in this
offering. In Jesus' name we pray. Amen.

*     *     *

God, we know that "offering" means giving all that we have and
are. Help us to do just that today. *So be it.*

*     *     *

O God, here is what we have. It is both visible and invisible. The
visible are these tokens of our work represented by coins and paper.
But the invisible is here too. We are offering the fragile dreams and
hopes by which we chart our lives. Receive them in love and bless
them to completion. Amen.

*     *     *

"Inasmuch as you have done it to one of the least of these, you have
done it to me." Help us, God, to see you in the needs that confront us

each day. Help us to see you in the poor, the hungry, the frightened, the lonely. As we offer ourselves to needy brothers and sisters may we know that we are touching you. Amen.

\*   \*   \*

You have given us so much, O God, and now we are attempting to return the favor. Our gifts are but pitiful symbols of the love we have for you. Receive them in this love and use them to further your caring in our world. Amen.

\*   \*   \*

"She gave all that she had." So Christ singled out for praise a poor widow who had given but a penny. As we make our offering today, help us to reflect on this woman's courage and what it would mean for us to do the same. Could it be that what God wants far more than our money is our total commitment to the way of love Christ died for? Jesus, too, gave all that he had. Can we do the same? Amen.

\*   \*   \*

You are amazing grace. You are unique, unrepeatable, a fragile miracle. You are God's grand and glorious gift. Gifts evoke gifts. And so we who are the gifts of creation now give gifts to our Creator. Let us give with the wild abandon that befits such examples of amazing grace. Amen.

\*   \*   \*

We come before you today, Father/Mother God, to present our gifts to you for the furthering of your love in the world. We do this in humility, knowing that we are the receivers, not the givers, of the greatest gift ever—Jesus Christ. Amen.

\*   \*   \*

God, may we give today not just feeble tokens of our work in the money we place in the offering baskets, but may we also place ourselves in these baskets in a new way, so that we leave this worship service renewed as your servants for our world. In the name of the one who was most fully a servant of all, Jesus Christ. Amen.

\*        \*        \*

O God, take these gifts we can all see, our money, but also receive what none of us can see, our time. Help us today to make a gift of time to you. In the name of the one who always had time even for the least of humanity, Jesus Christ. Amen.

\*        \*        \*

### Acts of Dedication

LEADER: Our message is that God was reconciling all persons through Christ, not counting their trespasses against them.

CONGREGATION: *And entrusting to us the message of reconciliation. So we are ambassadors for Christ; God appealing to needy humanity through us* (2 Cor. 5:19, 20, adapted). *In a broken world where we have nothing to lose but everything, we accept with humility and awe this invitation to be agents of Christ's reconciling love in the world.*

\*        \*        \*

LEADER: The God of all history needs and calls us to be agents of love. We are sent into the world to be concerned and caring people.

CONGREGATION: *Send us, God. Send us next door, into the next room, to speak somehow to a human heart beating alongside ours. Send us to be bearers of dignity in a subhuman, hopeless situation. Send us to show joy in a moment and a place where there has been no joy but only the will to die.*

*Send us to reflect your light in the darkness of futility, hopelessness, and the horror of human cruelty. But give us your light, too, God, in our own darkness and need. Amen.*

\*          \*          \*

LEADER: There is so much to be done. "Dedication" means deciding to be the one to do it.

CONGREGATION: *Because God loves us, we can know what it is to love others. Let us go forth boldly into the world, obediently, decisively, lovingly, joyfully, to bring God's peace and life to all.*

\*          \*          \*

LEADER: Christ Jesus, whose death and resurrection we remember, and whose second coming we await:

CONGREGATION: *With your help we will do our best*
*To say the word,*
*And do the work,*
*And be the person*
*In whom our neighbors may see*
*God's reign coming near*
*And God's holy love revealed.*

LEADER: Servants of Christ, the Savior Jesus accepts our honest intentions, and will give us the help we need to perform them faithfully.

CONGREGATION: *God help us to do so.*

\*          \*          \*

LEADER: Who are you?

Left: *We are the people who once were lost but now have been found.*
Right: *We have been found for a purpose. We have been given a job.*

CONGREGATION: *It is for us to love as we have been loved, to die as others have died for us.*

LEADER: Then go forth to your task in the knowledge of your acceptance before God; be present to life as it is given to you; and remember your obligation to all creation. In the name of God the Creator, Redeemer, and Sustainer. God be with you.

CONGREGATION: *And with your spirit.*

LEADER: Amen.

CONGREGATION: *Amen.*

\*     \*     \*

LEADER: This has been a good time, but has it really made any difference?

CONGREGATION: *We are the answers to this question. It is up to us whether we leave this service with renewed dedication to follow God's will or instead do nothing transforming for ourselves or our world. May we grasp the challenge and leave this place truly transformed as Christ-bearers in the world.*

\*     \*     \*

LEADER: Where do we go from here?

CONGREGATION: *We go home to continue "business as usual," but not quite. It is unusual for people to take time to worship. May we show that we are truly extra-ordinary people by how we live in our everyday situations, knowing that Christ is with us, seeing us through as faithful people who care about our world.*

\*     \*     \*

LEADER: Dedication means commitment. It means deciding to follow a particular course of action or thought. For Christians dedication means commitment to follow the way of Christ.

CONGREGATION: *But Christ's way is often hard and demanding. It ends in the cross.*

LEADER: Dedication means commitment to follow Christ's way no matter what. Do you have the courage to make such a dedication?

CONGREGATION: *We do with God as our helper, even though it means the cross. Christ's way of love and care is the only way to abundant life and joy.*

\*       \*       \*

LEADER: God is always on the side of the oppressed.

CONGREGATION: *We are only as near to God as we are far from the person or group or nation we like the least.*

LEADER: Our job is reconciliation with justice.

CONGREGATION: *It is not easy.*

LEADER: We will likely never see total victory in our lifetimes.

CONGREGATION: *But it is our job.*

LEADER: Go with God's blessing, knowing that no matter how rough the going, God's love and care are with you.

CONGREGATION: *Amen.*

\*       \*       \*

## Benedictions

LEADER: Go now, remembering what we have done here. Go, remembering that you are a forgiven people, eternally loved, thoughtfully instructed, gratefully obedient, responding, and responsible wherever you are. You can never be the same again.

CONGREGATION: *We know. We go to be God's people in the world.*

LEADER: May God's peace and joy go with you. So be it.

CONGREGATION: *So be it!*

\*       \*       \*

LEADER: Go forth now into a world where apathy and half-heartedness are dominant. Move the world a little. In the name of God the Creator, Redeemer, and Sustainer. God be with you.

CONGREGATION: *And with you.*
LEADER: Amen.
CONGREGATION: *Amen.*

\*       \*       \*

LEADER: With your love deep in our hearts,
CONGREGATION: *God go with us;*
LEADER: With your wisdom to know and understand,
CONGREGATION: *God go with us;*
LEADER: With your Spirit stirring in our souls,
CONGREGATION: *God go with us;*
LEADER: With your power to care and share in your world,
CONGREGATION: *God go with us to a new day. Amen.*

\*       \*       \*

LEADER: May God's grace, mercy, and strength be with you.
CONGREGATION: *And may we be instruments of God's grace, mercy, and strength to the world in which we live. Amen.*

\*       \*       \*

Go now in the confident knowledge that God gives you strength, hope, love, and peace. Alleluia!

\*       \*       \*

Now may you go with God into the sunlight of a new relationship in which you can be a light for people who are desperately searching for love and care. Amen.

\*       \*       \*

Today is the first day of the rest of your life and
The last day of the first of your life.
Live it as both a beginning and an end,
With the hope that new beginnings bring,

With the commitment that endings demand,
Knowing in all you do that God's love is with you,
Sustaining, supporting, encouraging. Amen.

\*          \*          \*

LEADER: God is a gentle God.
CONGREGATION: *We are to go forth with this gentleness in our lives.*
LEADER: God is a tender God.
CONGREGATION: *We shall be known as persons of tenderness.*
LEADER: God is a forgiving God.
CONGREGATION: *We are to bestow the gift of forgiveness in our relationships with others each day.*
LEADER: We are made in God's image.
CONGREGATION: *We are to be embodiers of God.*
LEADER: God is with you in this joyous, awe-filled commission.
CONGREGATION: *Amen.*

\*          \*          \*

Go now in peace, not in pieces. May God wrap you in wholeness, unity, and strength. May God give you the energy to face the hurts and challenges in this coming week with Christ's patient compassion. Amen.

\*          \*          \*

Reach out and touch your neighbor here at the service and give this person a tender, gentle, loving touch. This is what God wills for each of us—the tender kindness of a human touch—the language of love. Amen.

\*          \*          \*

LEADER: Take this truth home—God is with you.
CONGREGATION: *May our lives reflect this knowledge of God's presence in all we say and do.*

LEADER: God is with us, not as a zealous conscience demanding perfection, but as a loving parent wanting the best for us.

CONGREGATION: *Life is difficult, but we affirm that we have new strength and courage to go back into our daily lives because we know that God is with us. Amen.*

*   *   *

## Alternatives for the Doxology, Gloria Patri, Lord's Prayer, and Trinitarian Formula

We are often asked what to do about the Doxology, Gloria Patri, Lord's Prayer, and Trinitarian Formula, four liturgical texts used a great deal in contemporary worship services. Our first response is to ask the questioner to reflect on why these particular texts are used in their service. All four texts have a worthy and significant liturgical history, but we wonder if they need always be used. Do we not run the risk of "liturgical fundamentalism" if we insist that every service must contain certain texts? After all, Jesus did not say that we were to pray the Lord's Prayer at every worship service. He said instead that we are to pray "like this." We feel he was inviting new prayers based on his prayer. We wonder if he really feels honored that we repeat the same words over and over again at each service. Our first recommendation is therefore to consider eliminating these liturgical texts or other habitually used sexist texts from the worship service. If such elimination is not deemed wise, then two other alternatives are possible. First, you may want to use the texts as they are and announce or publish a statement in the bulletin that these texts represent a particular time in history when people were not aware of concerns for inclusive language. Second, you may want to devise alternatives to these texts using some of the same ideas, and in the case of the Doxology and Gloria Patri the same music, but different and inclusive words. We present some of these alternatives below. Note that it can be a most helpful experience to invite groups from your congregation to design their own alternatives to these texts, especially the Lord's Prayer. Such work can help a group wrestle with the real meaning of these texts and come to a much greater understanding of them.

## Doxology

### Original

Praise God, from whom all blessings flow;
Praise him, all creatures here below;
Praise him above, ye heavenly host;
Praise Father, Son, and Holy Ghost. Amen.

### Alternatives

Praise God, from whom all blessings flow;
Praise God, all creatures here below;
Praise God above, ye heavenly host;
Praise Maker, Christ, and Holy Ghost. Amen.

Praise God, from whom all blessings flow;
Praise God, our help in times of woe;
Praise God, our comforter and friend;
Praise God, who's with us in the end. Amen.

## Gloria Patri

### Original

Glory be to the Father and to the Son and to the Holy Ghost;
As it was in the beginning, is now, and ever shall be, world without end. Amen. Amen.

*Alternatives*

Glory be to our Maker and to the Christ and to the Holy Ghost;
As it was in the beginning, is now, and ever shall be, world without
end. Amen. Amen.

Glory be to our Yahweh and to Jesus and to the Holy Fire;
As it was in the beginning, is now, and ever shall be, world without
end. Amen. Amen.

## The Lord's Prayer

| *Original* | *Alternative* |
|---|---|
| Our Father, who art in heaven, | Our Mother/Father, who is everywhere, |
| Hallowed be Thy name. | Holy be your names. |
| Thy kingdom come, | May your new age come |
| Thy will be done, | May your will be done |
| On earth, as it is in heaven. | In this and in every time and place. |
| Give us this day our daily bread, | Meet our needs each day and |
| And forgive us our debts, | Forgive our failure to love |
| As we forgive our debtors. | As we forgive this same failure in others. |
| And lead us not into temptation, | Save us in hard times, and |
| But deliver us from evil. | Lead us into the ways of love. |
| For Thine is the kingdom, and the power, | For yours is the wholeness, and the power, |
| And the glory, forever. Amen. | And the loving, forever. Amen. |

## Trinitarian Formula

Here, especially, many persons object to any changes of language. We believe limited use of the traditional Trinitarian formula may be appropriate as long as this usage is balanced by other, feminine references to God. Objections to changing the formula are usually for either historical or theological reasons or both. Historically, the formula is a solid part of our tradition. It has become a unifying basis on which Christian denominations perform baptism, for example. Changes of this formula by some denominations and not by others might jeopardize the transdenominational acceptance of baptisms, it is argued. It is also argued that it is impossible to find substitute nonsexist words for the Trinitarian formula that are not in themselves limited in what they say. Many suggested substitutes use descriptive words for the three persons of the Trinity rather than the traditional names for God that are used in the original formula. These descriptive words tend to limit our view of that aspect of God to that particular function. "Father" is more inclusive than "Creator," it is argued, because the term "Father" includes many more descriptive realities than "Creator." There is some truth in these arguments, although they certainly do not persuade us. We continue to feel that generally it is important to use an alternative form of the Trinitarian formula if it is used at all. We feel that many of these alternatives, while perhaps being more specifically descriptive, also contain words that help us discover new understandings of the meaning of the Trinity.

| *Original* | *Alternatives* |
|---|---|
| Father, Son, Holy Spirit (Ghost) | Maker (Creator), Christ (Jesus), Holy Spirit |
| | Creator, Redeemer, Sustainer |
| | Creator, Savior, Healer |
| | Source, Servant, Guide |
| | Three in One, One in Three |

# 8. Liberated Services

The services that follow are complete in that they give specific suggestions for every part of a service developed around a specific theme. However, they are included here only as examples of what can be done in liberating the liturgy. They are for your use, and that means you should feel free to adapt them to your own particular situation and your own special liturgical style.

We have tried to list a variety of available hymns, both traditional and contemporary. All of the traditional hymns are found in *The Book of Hymns* of the United Methodist Church and in other traditional hymn books. We have also listed hymns from *Sisters and Brothers, Sing!* and *Everflowing Streams* (see Appendix C). In some cases, we have rewritten sexist hymns or added new words to an old tune, and here we have included the new words for your use.

Part of liberating the liturgy, as we have said, is to see new possibilities for our old forms. This is true in every section of the liturgy, but perhaps especially in the sermon. Thus, we have included suggestions for very nontraditional sermons. If these seem unusable in your particular situation, certainly the same ideas can be incorporated into a more traditional sermon. We hope, however, you'll seriously consider the possibility of trying something new with the sermon and with other parts of the liturgy. Our suggestions here are only a feeble beginning for what you and your friends can do if you let your imaginations loose. We hope you'll do just that.

## Finding Acceptance and Self-Worth from God

### *Prelude*

Songs emphasizing our need for acceptance and self-worth such as "I Am, . . ." "I Gotta Be Me," et cetera.

### *Call to Worship*

LEADER: We come to this service with so many needs and longings. We've been many different places, conceived many different thoughts.

CONGREGATION: *But underneath all our differences is the same basic need for love and acceptance.*

LEADER: And that's why we're here—to admit to each other our need for love,

CONGREGATION: *And to celebrate the most marvelous fact of the universe—that God loves us and accepts us just as we are. Alleluia!*

### *Hymn*

"Love Divine, All Loves Excelling"; or "We Are Gathered," no. 12, *Sisters and Brothers, Sing!*; or "God Makes All Things New," no. 75, *Everflowing Streams.*

### *Invocation*

God, you are both heavenly Father and Mother to us and we know you are with us at all times. But we pause to ask early in this service that your Spirit of love especially surround and invade us as we worship here today. We really want to know you, God. Be with us now. Amen.

## Call to Confession

To be open to God we must be honest with ourselves no matter how painful or distasteful this may be. We have missed the mark of our high calling. Let us confess this to God.

## General Prayer of Confession
### (Prayed by all)

Sometimes we feel hopeless and afraid, God. Does anyone really care about us? Do our lives really make any difference when we look at the whole universe—when we see so many other people who are more talented, rich, and famous than we? Sometimes too, the fact of our own impending death sinks into us, and we're scared. Is there eternal life? If there is, what's it like? Why can't we trust you that everything will be okay no matter what? And yet all the nagging doubts about death and life are still there. Forgive us for our doubts and fears, God. We know that often they make us treat others cruelly. Forgive us for all the evil we've done to others in the name of our own anxieties. In Jesus' name, Amen.

## Words of Assurance

LEADER: A sparrow falters.
CONGREGATION: *Life goes on.*
LEADER: A sparrow falls.
CONGREGATION: *Creation's castoff.*
LEADER: Yet forever received and affirmed.
CONGREGATION: *Even the sparrow finds a home.*
LEADER: You are accepted.
CONGREGATION: *Accepted by that which is greater than ourselves.*
LEADER: Do not ask for the name now.

CONGREGATION: *Do not try to do anything now.*

LEADER: Do not seek for anything, perform anything, intend anything.

CONGREGATION: *Simply accept the fact that we are accepted.*

LEADER: Forever received and affirmed.

CONGREGATION: *Even the sparrow finds a home.*

## Scripture Readings

*Old Testament:* A paraphrase of Psalm 8

O God, our God,
Your greatness is seen in all the world!

Your glory reaches to the heavens,
Even children and babies sing your praise.
You have built a fortress because of your foes, to still the enemy and the revengeful.

When I look at the sky, the work of your fingers,
At the moon and the stars, which you have made—
What are we, that you think of us;
And our children, that you should care for them?

Yet you made us but a little less than you yourself;
And you crowned us with glory and honor!
You made us rulers over all you have made;
You gave us responsibility for all things:
    sheep and cattle, and wild animals too;
    the birds and the fish,
    and all the creatures in the seas.
God, our God,
    your greatness is seen in all the world.

*New Testament:* Matthew 25:14–30

### Affirmation of Faith

We believe in the infinite worth of every human being. We believe that our worth is ultimately derived not by what others think of us or even by what we think of ourselves, but by what God thinks of us. We affirm that God loves each of us with a richness and depth that is beyond our wildest imaginings.

We believe that every human being falters and fails at times and needs the forgiving love of God to keep going. We know that each of us becomes deadened to our world and our brothers and sisters, and so we need the enlivening power of God's Holy Spirit to be with us bringing us alive inside.

Each of us faces the terrifying unknown we call death. And that is why God's promise of eternal life sealed in Jesus holds out so much hope to us. We know that, even though our lives may be filled with great trouble and sorrow, God never deserts us, never gives up on us. With this faith firm in our hearts we can shout with the saints of all the ages: Alleluia!

### New Ways of Doing a Sermon

[1. You may want to have three persons from your community who have struggled with the questions of acceptance and self-worth share with the community what has happened to them on their journey through life. If there is time, you might then want to divide the congregation into small groups so they can react to what was said and share some of their own personal struggles.

2. You might like to divide your congregation into small groups and let them sculpture from junk materials (clay, paper, rubber bands, ballons, paper clips, toothpicks, scraps of cloth, whatever you have available) their response as a small group to the words of assurance or the affirmation of faith. They could then bring their finished

creations forward as part of the offering, and, if you have time, you might want a spokesperson from each group to share with everyone some of the group's thinking as they made what they did.

3. You might want to ask a small group from your congregation to work ahead of time on acting out a contemporary version of the New Testament lesson. This could then be presented as the sermon and comments solicited from the congregation and/or the minister.

4. If you have some persons in your group who are skilled dancers, you may want to ask them to do a dance based on the paraphrase of Psalm 8. This too could be an effective part of a sermon.

Remember, if you pick either of the last two alternatives, try to ask the people who are going to work on them in plenty of time so that there will not be undue pressure on them. Even several months early is not too soon.]


### Hymn

"O Thou Who Art the Shepherd" (you will want to change the word "Father" in verse two to "God"); or "Magic Penny," no. 124, *Sisters and Brothers, Sing*; or "Creator God, Who frees us to Create," no. 58, *Everflowing Streams*.


### Offertory Prayer

God, money is important, but sometimes we get to thinking that it's the most important thing in the world. We know that's not true, God, and that thinking like that can destroy us if we're not careful. Help us now to make an honest gift of our money and of ourselves in the service of your love. Amen.

[The offering is an ideal time to have a sharing of joys and concerns from the community. The apostle Paul says that the church should be the kind of community where we weep with those who weep and rejoice with those who rejoice. But in order to do this we need to know the special things in people's hearts. In a small congregation this sharing can be spontaneous. Led by the minister or a lay person, the congregation is simply invited to share some of their special joys and concerns from the past week. This can be a beautiful community-building experience. Afterward, a time of silence can be observed when these concerns and joys along with others that were not expressed are brought before God in prayer. Or the minister or a lay person can pray aloud a spontaneous prayer that incorporates these joys and concerns of the community. If the congregation is large, it may be necessary to ask certain persons to serve as representatives of the total congregation to come before the whole group and share particular joys and concerns they have had this week or that they know others have experienced during the week. Different persons should do this each week and all those who do it should be encouraged to keep their presentations brief. The purpose is not to preach a sermon or give a long history, but simply to state a joy or concern that has been experienced by someone in the congregation.

Another way to do the offering is to have the congregation process around the church to place their money offering in strategically located baskets while singing an offertory song such as the one at the end of this suggested service. Such physical movement is often good. It impresses upon everyone that the offering is not just dropping some money in a plate as it comes by, but that it involves the presenting of your whole body to God.]

### Act of Dedication

LEADER: "People who need people are the luckiest people in the world."

CONGREGATION: *We need people and people need us.*

LEADER: To be a Christian is to be alive to these needs in ourselves
and others and respond to them.

CONGREGATION: *Well, let's get busy!*

## Hymn

"Take My Life and Let It Be Consecrated"; or "This Is My Gift," no.
99, *Sisters and Brothers, Sing!*; or "Vision for Tomorrow, Action for
Today," no. 76, *Everflowing Streams.*

## Benediction

[Instead of a spoken benediction, let each person turn to his or her
neighbor and affirm that person with a handshake and one word
that means acceptance to himself or herself.]

\*       \*       \*

## Celebrating God

### For Your Meditation

How do you imagine God? What image do you have? Could it be
that God's aliveness is not static, but moving? Could God also be in
process, continually becoming? How could God be anything else if
God loves us? Love implies process, the capacity to change with the
needs of the person who is loved. To imagine God then, we need
moving images—kinetic sculpture, film, multiple images, and colors. As Buckminster Fuller says, "For God, to me, it seems is a verb,
not a noun."

### Call to Worship

LEADER: Welcome to an adventure that can be the most exciting
adventure of your life.

CONGREGATION: *But we came to a worship service.*

LEADER: Worship is an adventure, for in worship we attempt to be in communion with One of whom we can know something, but whom we cannot wholly know.

CONGREGATION: *Even while we experience God's presence we know that there are other dimensions of God we have not yet experienced.*

LEADER: God is like the horizon. We see the horizon, we experience it, but when we get there it's always out beyond us.

CONGREGATION: *So let us give ourselves totally today to worshipping the beyond in our midst.*

## Hymn

"Immortal, Invisible, God Only Wise" (substitute "Mother" for "Father" when it is used for the second time in verse 4); or "Thank God," no. 14 *Sisters and Brothers, Sing!*; or "O How Glorious, Full of Wonder," no. 10, *Everflowing Streams.*

## Invocation

God, we pray that your spirit may fill our spirits today so that we come alive in new ways to your reality. Amen.

## Call to Confession

[Read some newspaper headlines and follow with this statement.]

The world is in agony and although we know we are by no means responsible for all the world's sorrow, we also know that we have added to it by what we have done and failed to do. Let us confess our sins before God.

## General Prayer of Confession

God, we come before you today aching inside. We are revolted by the news that comes to us daily of hatred and war. But we are doubly troubled today because we know that the awful things we see going on in the world are also inside of us to one degree or another. We know, too, God, that often we have tried to go our lives alone without calling on your help. We haven't even been willing to take the time to see how an expanded concept of you might bring us to a brand new way of envisioning possibilities for ourselves. We need to experience today the radical, sweeping power of your active love in the midst of our halting and hesitant living. Amen.

## Words of Assurance

Look around you—God's powerful love is present in persons who
    care about you and about social justice for the world.
Look within you—God's powerful love is present in all your yearn-
    ings to be the very best person you possibly can be.

## Hymn

"Questions" (Tune: "Lonesome Valley")

We have come to ask some questions,
We have to ask them by ourselves.
Oh, nobody else can ask them for us.
We have to ask them for ourselves.

How can we begin to find God,
When God is so beyond our grasp?
Oh, when will we know God fully present?
This is the question we must ask.

Now we see with cloudy vision
What we'll know when we shall die.
Yet we can see now fantastic glimpses
Of God's strong love for which we cry.

So let us keep our questions coming,
Let us be bold to ask them clear.
For searching we find tremendous insight
Into God's love that's present here.

## Scripture Readings

*Old Testament:* Isaiah 42:10–17
*New Testament:* Luke 15:8–10
[Note that the first passage compares God to both a man and a woman. The second pictures God as a woman and is part of a trilogy of analogies that portrays God as both a man and a woman.]

## New Ways of Doing a Sermon

[You might want to send out a group from your church, a few weeks before this service, with cassette recorders to interview persons on the street with the question, "What do you think God is like?" A committee could then edit these comments down to about five minutes of the most interesting and this could be used to kick off dicussion about who God is. Youth groups might be especially excited by such a project. After the tape presentation perhaps the minister and someone of the opposite sex could do a dialogue reflecting on the nature of God. Such a dialogue might be open-ended with time for questions and comments from the congregation. You might also want to divide your congregation into several small discussion groups which could tackle various questions about God such as: Is it proper to think of God anthropomorphically as either male or female? (Note

that the Scripture passages mentioned above see God as female.)
What does it mean to say God is a verb? Is it valuable to conceive of
God as an active force rather than as a person? Do you like this way of
thinking? Are there ways of preserving the meaning of the concept of
God as Father without being sexist? What are they? After the groups
have batted these questions around a bit, they could then come
together and share some of their insights with the total group. The
minister or someone else would want to help direct this sharing and
perhaps add some comments of his or her own.

It would also be possible to begin the whole service by passing out
a short questionnaire on which provocative statements about God
were placed along with blanks for persons to check if they agree,
disagree, or are neutral about each statement. The sermon could
then be a group discussion of these statements or, if this does not
seem feasible, the minister could develop his or her sermon around
what the statements on the questionnaire told him or her about
God.

Another alternative would be to show the short (two-minute)
film "The Vision" (see Appendix C). This film presents the concept
of expanding our images of God by seeing God as feminine as well as
masculine through a visual joke. It is a good discussion starter and
comes with a complete guide which includes various ways of developing the discussion. The film could be shown, discussion in small
groups could take place, then the film could be shown again or the
pastor could make closing comments.

Still another alternative would be to ask some of the members of
your younger children's church school classes to draw a picture of
God. You could then make slides of these pictures and show them at
the beginning of the sermon to give persons a child's eye view of
God. Discussion, dialogue, or a straight monologue sermon could
then flow from these pictures.]

### Offertory Prayer

God, we know that all we have comes from you, but these gifts are made for spending, not for hoarding. So now as we share some of our material wealth, help us also to share all our talents as agents of your love in the world. Amen.

[The same suggestions made in the offering section of the service "Finding Acceptance and Self-Worth from God" would be appropriate here.]

### Hymn

"God, That Madest Earth and Heaven"; or "Who Knows the Face of God," no. 75, *Sisters and Brothers, Sing!*; or "Hearts Open Slowly," no. 18, *Everflowing Streams*.

### Benediction
*(Adapted from an ancient Navajo benediction)*

God is before us.
God is behind us.
God is above us.
God is below us.
God's words shall come from our mouths
For we are God's essence, a sign of God's love.
All is finished in beauty
All is finished in beauty
All is finished in beauty
All is finished in beauty.

\*       \*       \*

## Celebrating Liberation from Role Stereotypes

*A Service of Holy Commmunion*

### Call to Worship

LEADER: Christ's love is a liberating love.

CONGREGATION: *It sets us free to be the beautiful people we can be.*

LEADER: In worship we come together to celebrate and call upon Christ's liberating power for our lives.

CONGREGATION: *To be free is to be our own person and to know that the basic power of the universe which we call God is all for us in our struggle to be our best.*

### Hymn

"In Christ There Is No East or West" (change the last line of verse 2 to read "That binds all hu-man-kind." Verse 3 should be changed to the following:

> Join hands, then, friends of the faith,
> What-e'er your race may be.
> Who serves the God of life and love
> Is sure-ly kin to me.)

Or "Male and Female," no. 13, *Sisters and Brothers, Sing!*"; or "In Christ There Is No East or West" (paraphrased), no. 40, *Everflowing Streams.*

### Invocation

God, may the freeing power of your Spirit be with us in this service so that we are made restless to strive for liberation from old role stereotypes and old sins. Amen.

## Call to Confession

We can only be free to be new people when we face the past honestly and admit our wrongs. Let's do that now.

## General Prayer of Confession

MEN: We confess, O God, that our treatment of women has brought much suffering and hurt. For our temptation to treat women as objects for our own selfish lust, we ask your forgiveness, O God. For our tendency to feel threatened by women who are more intelligent and/or more aggressive than we are, we ask your help, God. For our attempts to shove women into narrow roles which may or may not be what they wish for their lives, we ask your pardon.

WOMEN: We, too, have much to confess, God. For our temptation to allow men to take roles of responsibility so that we may sit back and criticize, we ask your forgiveness, O God. For our tendency to play dumb or to be deceptive to get our way, we ask your help, God. For our efforts sometimes to imitate the "success" styles of men, even when we know they are empty husks of truth, we ask your pardon.

ALL: We admit in shame that we have not lived and loved as we should have. Help us to see the shining truth of your love in each person. May we go beyond stereotypes to see one another in depth and beauty. Amen.

## Words of Assurance

WOMEN: We have heard your confession and we assure you that God has also heard. In the Spirit of God's loving care, we proclaim that you are forgiven. Take up your life and walk!

MEN: We have heard your confession and we assure you that God has also heard. In the Spirit of God's loving care, we proclaim that you are forgiven. Take up your life and walk!

## Doxology

"Praise God, from Whom All Blessings Flow"
(Use either the traditional "Old 100th" hymn tune or a new tune such as the one by Avery and Marsh in *Songbook for Saints and Sinners*. The words could be either of the paraphrases shown in Chapter 7.)

## Scripture Readings

*Old Testament:* Genesis 1:26–31
*New Testament:* Galatians 3:23–28

## New Ways of Doing a Sermon

[The sermon could take many forms. It could be a straight exposition on the Scripture passages, drawing from them God's concern that each of us be full human beings seen beyond any particular roles imposed upon us by society or ourselves. The sermon could also be a dialogue betwen a man and a woman in which they share what the Scripture passages mean to them and how they have begun to achieve liberation from role stereotypes. Part of the sermon could be an impromptu drama showing some of the tragic humor of our role stereotyping. Some excellent plays and articles have been written that help us to see how ridiculous some of our roles are today. Naturally, if a play is done, you'll have to do advance preparation with your actors. It need not be a production of professional quality, however, but simply good enough to get its point across with humor

and clarity. You might also want to show the film "Anything You
Want to Be" (see Appendix C). This short film shows how much a
young girl's vocational aspirations are influenced and shaped by the
roles women are expected to play. After the film, comments could be
made relating it to the whole question of role enslavement and the
Christian call to liberation. Also small group discussion could be a
part of reaction to this film or to any of the other means suggested for
doing the sermon.]

### Hymn

"Bread of the World"; or "Re-Member Me," no. 86, *Sisters and
Brothers, Sing!*; or "Give Thanks to God, The Source of Life," no.
49, *Everflowing Streams*.

[As this hymn is being sung representatives of the congregation
should bring the Communion elements forward and place them on
the worship table. After the hymn the minister lifts the bread and
wine.]

MINISTER: The gifts of God for the people of God.

MINISTER (lifting the loaf of bread as he or she breaks it): Christ's
body was broken so that we might be whole.

MINISTER (lifting the wine): Christ's blood was shed so that we might
be transfused with God's love.

[Try to make the way you serve Communion demonstrate what you
are trying to communicate about the liberating power of God's love.
If we really mean that this love breaks down role stereotypes, then we
should be willing to let all Christians serve one another in Communion. This is essentially what already happens in churches where
Communion is taken in the pews. But even if it is taken by coming
forward, still the "priesthood of all believers" should allow us to
serve one another. If there is room, you might want to ask persons to

come forward in small groups and stand together in a circle, each serving his or her neighbor the elements. By having small groups come forward and sit together at a table, you could achieve the same purpose. You may want to have special music during the receiving of Communion. You may want to have persons receive it in silence. You may want to have them say their own words of love and care to one another as they serve each other. Each congregation and each physical setting is different, so it will be up to you to come up with the most effective way of sharing Communion together. You may want to encourage people to bring their offerings as they come forward to take Communion, or you may want to have the offering at another time.]

### Prayer of Thanksgiving
*(Prayed by all)*

God, our human history is a record of your love for us. Many years ago our ancestors in the faith were called by you to celebrate the Passover to remember how you rescued your people from slavery. Today we have celebrated a new Passover and a new covenant as in this Communion we remember Christ's loving death for us all. We know this death, too, is a freeing from slavery not just of a political nature but of all kinds. In this service we are especially grateful to you for calling us to a responsible freedom that goes beyond all kinds of role stereotypes. In Christ's name we pray. Amen.

### Hymn

To tunes no. 5 and no. 294, "I Love Thy Kingdom, Lord," in *The Book of Hymns* (United Methodist), words by Martha Montague Wilson:

Yes, all are one in Christ,
Whose one baptism share;
Not Jew or Gentile, slave or free,
Not male or female be.

In Christ all barriers fall,
One people—all are we;
The children of bright promises,
Christ comes to make us free.

The gift of life we share,
The chains of slavery fall;
And women, men, from every land,
Give answer to Christ's call.

So stand in Christ and live,
The life of faith and love;
Sing: All are one in Christ,
Who leads to joy here and above.


### Benediction

The Passing of the Peace.

[Have each person greet her or his neighbor with a handshake and an embrace and these words: "The peace of God go with you my sister (brother)." The response: "And with you my brother (sister)."]

\*       \*       \*


## A Wedding Service

A whole book could be done, and we understand some are in the making, to deal with the wedding service. This is not the place for such a book, but a few comments are essential. First, it is important to realize that the Church only got into the wedding ceremony fairly recently. Marriage was a wholly civil ceremony until about the tenth century. Thus many of the customs we still find in today's ceremonies are totally pagan and come down to us from a time when women were considered the property of men. The "giving away of the bride" by her father, for example, is a throwback to the old custom when the bride was sold to the prospective groom. Some attempts have been made to redeem this part of the traditional wedding ceremony by reinterpreting it to mean that this giving away of the bride is symbolic of the blessing the parents of the families bestow upon the new couple. If this is an appropriate interpretation, however, why isn't the symbolism more in line with it? You'll note that in our service the parental blessing is obvious and the giving away of the bride is eliminated.

More and more ministers are encouraging couples to write their own services. We see this as a healthy sign when it is done with real care and with the help of someone skilled in liturgy, such as the minister. It is important for couples who are attempting to write their own service to realize that they do not have to come up with an all new service. Sections from other contemporary services may speak to them and they will want to use them. Also parts of the traditional service may still be what they want to use. The vows of many traditional services have power and poetry that make them effective even in a service that is largely contemporary.

We believe that a wedding service is especially for the couple to be married and that their tastes should govern how the service is developed. We should not attempt to impose our musical or poetic tastes upon them. We do have a responsibility to help them have a theologically and socially responsible service, however. It is hoped that persons can use the service that follows as a guide to give them ideas as they develop their own wedding service.

## The Service of Worship

## Celebrating the Marriage

OF

_____

(name of bride)

*and*

_____

(name of groom)

_____

(the date)

### Prelude

[Whatever musical style is especially meaningful to the couple should be used during the service.]

### Call to Worship

MINISTER: On this special day we gather for this special service to celebrate the wedding of two special people.
CONGREGATION: *This is a day for singing and rejoicing.*
MINISTER: Alleluia, praise to God.
CONGREGATION: *Alleluia, praise to God!*

### Processional

[Both bride and groom come in gaily together, along with their especially close friends and relatives. As they come in everyone sings the hymn.]

## Hymn

"Together," no. 161, *Sisters and Brothers, Sing!*

## Invocation

Gracious God, may your spirit inform and inspire this service of worship, and may it always guide the two who are to be joined in marriage today and all of us here who witness this event. Amen.

## Call to Confession

Even at times of exquisite happiness like this we must be reminded that we *know* better than we *do*. Let us confess our sins before God.

## General Prayer of Confession

God, this is a service celebrating love and so we are reminded of how often we have failed to be loving; celebrating the creation of a new family and so we remember how often we have taken our own families for granted and failed to see possibilities for fulfillment in them. Two people today are pledging themselves to be "all for" each other, and yet our lives are strewn with pledges seriously made and then lightly broken. We have not loved as we should have; we have not been with and for our families as we could have, and too often we have been untrue to our commitments. May our participation in the creation of this new relationship help us to re-examine and then renew all our relationships through Jesus Christ our Lord. Amen.

## Words of Assurance

The God who created us can re-create us. This is the truth that sets us free.

### Scripture Readings

*Old Testament:* Psalm 150
*New Testament:* 1 Corinthians 13

### Contemporary Reading

[A passage from some contemporary writing that has been especially meaningful to the couple is read.]

### Sermon Meditation

[Here the minister performing the ceremony could be invited to share some of his or her insights about the meaning of marriage or of a particular word or phrase in the marriage covenant. This might also be a time when the couple themselves would want to share with the assembled group some of their understandings about marriage and life in general.]

### The Covenant of Marriage

[Where blanks are given for the names of the bride and groom, it is appropriate to alternate the order in which they appear.]

### Opening Remarks

This is it, a moment packed with anticipation, when standing before God and this group of friends and relatives _____ and _____ pledge themselves to one another in the covenant of marriage.

We hope that those of you who are married will take this occasion to renew your own vows, and that all of you will share in this celebration by offering your own personal prayers for this couple ready to begin a new life together.

### The Charge to the Bride and Groom

To the Christian, marriage is neither a casual nor a socially legislated business arrangement. It is a holy covenant between two persons who love each other. _____ and _____ , your marriage is one of the most sacred and most treasured parts of your life. It is a celebration of all the mystery and wonder that deep love brings to living. It is also a recognition, however, that love and marriage are not always easy and that along with the tenderness, newness, and joy in a marriage, a marriage must overcome many forces that might destroy it. Love is dynamic and will fly away from a marriage that has become static and unbending. When love lives, as it does here today, it reflects the deepest and most tender secrets of the universe.

And I charge you, _____, and you, _____, with the responsibility to keep alive; to grow, to change, to maintain the capacity for wonder, for spontaneity, for humor; to remain flexible, warm, and sensitive. Give fully to each other, show your real feelings to one another, save time for each other, no matter what demands are made upon your day. I charge you to nurture each other to fullness and wholeness, realizing that each of you will need at times to bring strength and support and worth to the other. I charge you, as you grow to love each other more deeply, to discover out of this love a love for all of creation in which the mystery of your love has happened.

## The Questions

[The bride and groom shall each be asked the following questions, which should be answered in the appropriate affirmative.]

Do you find within you a special love for _____ that convinces you that you want to spend the rest of your lives together?

Do you find within you the courage to resist the many deaths by which love can die?

Are you willing to love _____ into his/her unique fullness and to take the risk and accept the vulnerability of love again and again and again?

## The Blessing of the Families

MINISTER: Who give their blessing to this marriage and in the giving say an enthusiastic "Yes!" to this new relationship?

FAMILIES: *We do. Yes! Amen.*

## The Wedding Vows

[The bride and groom face each other; each makes his or her offering to the other, feeling free to add personal comments to the vows.]

I offer my love; I offer my strength; I offer my support; I offer my loyalty; I offer my faith; I offer my hope—in all the changing circumstances of life—as long as we both shall live.

## The Giving of the Rings

MINISTER: What symbols do you bring as evidence of the vows you have just taken?

THE COUPLE: *These rings.*

MINISTER: These rings mark the beginning of a life journey together filled with wonder, surprises, laughter, tears, celebration, grief, and joy. May these rings be a sign to you of the continuing love you have pledged to one another today.

[If the congregation attending the wedding is small enough, the couple may wish to pass their wedding rings around to the worshippers. Each person is asked to make a silent prayer for the couple as he or she touches these tokens of their love with her or his fingers. In this way the whole congregation can actively participate in the blessing of the rings.]

[The bride and groom face each other; each places the ring on the other's finger and says these words.]

I give you this sign of my love, knowing that love is precious and fragile, yet strong. Whenever I see your ring I will remember all that I have pledged to you here this day.

### The Response of the Congregation

As members of Christ's Church, we rejoice with you in the covenant you have made. We pledge to support and strengthen your life together, to speak the truth to you in love, and with you to seek to live a life of love for others.

### A Prayer

O God, we pray that this couple and all who are gathered here will grow in the understanding and experience of love. As _____ and _____ become bound closer to each other, may they also ever be more surely themselves. To your tender and watchful care we here commit ___ and ___ . In health and sickness, in abundance and want, in life and death, abide with them that they shall never withdraw from you. Through Jesus Christ. Amen.

## The Declaration

You have now publicly shared your love for and special commitment
to one another. Explore this love well with deep reverence. Explore it
with joy and hope and perseverance. I now pronounce you husband
and wife, according to the Spirit and in accord with human law.

## Benediction

Today is a new beginning in the lives of  _____
and  _____ . May God's peace and love go with
them as they continue life's journey. Amen.

## Recessional

"Morning Has Broken" (to be sung by all as the wedding party
leaves).

## Postlude

[Something joyful!]

# 9. How to Handle Objections to Changes in Your Service

Perhaps this chapter should have been entitled "How to Introduce Changes into Your Worship Service in Such a Way That Objections Never Materialize." Certainly the first way to handle objections should be to prevent them from ever occurring. But how do we do that?

What follows are some guidelines we have found helpful in working with congregations experiencing change in their worship. What we say is necessarily rather general and will need to be adapted or perhaps totally changed by you as you assess your particular situation. For some of you, our ideas may seem old hat or simply common sense. For us, many of them came out of arduous and sometimes quite painful experiences. We hope they are helpful to you.

The first rule in all communication, and especially communication concerned with bringing about change within a community, is to love and accept the other persons for who they are. No matter how right we are, if we present our arguments from a standpoint of superiority, we are in trouble from the start. All of us have probably known persons who were tremendously intelligent and often had great ideas, but who could never get anyone to agree with them. Their manner of presenting their concepts automatically made people want to argue with them. They seemed so cocky, so sure, so "know-it-all." That's a sure way to get into trouble in communication.

To communicate in love means to listen with your whole being to the other person. It means to attempt to hear what that person is really saying, not just with his or her words but also by the meaning and feeling behind those words.

To communicate in love means to accept the other person even though we may disagree completely with what she or he believes. It means being willing to take time with the other person and build up a trusting relationship with that person.

Unless your community of faith is extremely small, it will be impossible for you to do all this communicating in love by yourself. You will need to train others to help you so that persons in your community can have a chance to express themselves personally on this issue. In churches with large memberships you will need to be a resource to the resource persons. But no matter what the size of the situation, the basic strategy of communicating in love personally with others in your community must remain.

Even a concern to communicate with others in love and acceptance will not prevail by itself. Coupled with this must be a clear and rational presentation of what sexism is and does. The earlier chapters in this book should help you develop such a rationale.

Someone has said that a group will accept anything if it's explained the right way. That may be a bit of an exaggeration, but it is far more true than most of us realize. To explain something in the right way generally means to use all the channels of communication open to you. This means that in addition to small study groups and one-to-one dialogue on sexism and worship, informative articles about the subject should occasionally appear in your church's newsletter and sermons should sometimes deal specifically with this issue or at least make passing reference to it. Organized groups within the church should be encouraged to tackle the issue and have several discussion groups work on it.

It is important to approach all these channels of communication with great sensitivity, however. It does much more harm than good to have a group deal negatively with the issue. It should only be brought up in a group when you feel a sufficient number of people have their levels of awareness raised to bring about a positive discussion of the issue. Articles in your newsletter and comments in sermons should also be handled with great sensitivity. It is important not to overkill with constant references to the subject. It is also good to vary your approach to the subject so that sometimes you talk of how women feel in sexist services while at other times you point out ways of interpreting many of the sexist passages of the Bible or discuss new concepts of God.

It is also important to recognize that it may be necessary to move gradually in bringing actual changes to your worship services. Throughout this book we have suggested that such a gradual approach may be the best strategy in most congregations.

To move gradually to eliminate sexism in worship may mean that at first you simply take out all obviously sexist references in your worship: You stop using hymns and prayers that refer to man and mankind, brothers, sons, and so on. This need not be especially difficult since there are many excellent prayers and hymns that are already nonsexist, as we have noted earlier (see also Appendix A). When talking of God you simply use the word "God" or a nonsexist synonym such as "Creator" rather than a sexist word like "Father" or even the pronoun "He." The same careful use of words should be followed in the sermon.

Only after some real communication has had a chance to happen, in small groups and on a one-to-one basis, will you want to move on to occasionally bringing both the masculine and the feminine attributes into the service with references to God as "Mother/Father," or "She/He."

You will want also to liberate your worship in ways other than simply by the use of language. We have talked of liberating the leadership of the liturgy and how essential this is; it is important to pick the persons who will be leading in a new way with great care. They should be persons who are highly respected in your faith community. You should be willing to spend time with them (or have another knowledgeable person spend time with them) so that they do an outstanding job of leading worship—better than what has been done.

You may also want to introduce other changes that will help free your services and make them more meaningful for the congregation as a whole. New music, the use of film and dance, discussion sermons, and so forth, may be things you'll want to try. Be careful, however, that you don't overwhelm your congregation with change. You may end up having your people identifying nonsexist worship with a particular type of music or sermon, and that would be most unfortunate.

On the other hand, sometimes introducing several changes at once can help with the acceptance of each of the changes. For example, if you know that your congregation wants a different kind of music, you might introduce that at the same time you begin nonsexist services. The congregation would then be much more likely to be receptive to the nonsexist change too.

This principle can be stated in a simple rule: *Where possible, mix a popular and unpopular change together to achieve maximum acceptance of the unpopular change.*

A second important principle is: *Where possible, introduce something new by showing that it has elements of the familiar within it.*

For example, if you want to introduce a new songbook into your congregation, you can best do this your first Sunday by singing a song from the book that you know your people like very much. They will then feel much better toward the new book which they might have rejected completely had you introduced it with a totally unfamiliar song.

As you work with the people in your congregation, do not let some of them persuade you that doing nothing is moving gradually ahead. It may be extremely important to move slowly in bringing about liturgical change, but you should always be able to point to some progress, some work that is being done. Often the opponents of change attempt to neutralize the changers by convincing them they are progressing when nothing is being done. That is false and should be rejected firmly by you.

No matter how carefully you engineer your program of change, you will probably run into some persons who are against it. It is important to listen to these persons and try to discover why they are opposed to the changes. With careful listening you may learn about some of the problems in your own techniques in working for change. This can help you as you continue your work. You may also discover that the persons who are objecting do so for reasons that are often quite nonrational. The individuals may cover their objections with seemingly rational reasons or by appealing to numbers ("So many people are upset in our church now"). But when these arguments are shown to be ineffective, these persons may still continue to object, always trying to find a new rationalization. Often such objection springs from a deep nostalgia, a worship of the past when everything was stable and everyone seemed happy. Such persons often say, "The worship service was the one stable rock I had to cling to, and now you want to take that away too."

Try to help these persons know that you understand some of their deep feelings and fears. Perhaps you may restate their ideas to make sure you understand what they are saying and feeling and so that they will know that you understand. Then try to help them realize that liberating the liturgy won't destroy their faith but will actually help to make it more solid. It will also be a powerful way of helping others who are now turned off by worship languages and practices to discover a strong and viable faith. Such appeals to the new strength that the objecting person can find in a changed liturgy and to the sacrifice that these persons can make to help others can be powerfully convincing.

No matter what you do or say, however, you must be prepared to accept the fact that perhaps some people will be so turned off by change in the liturgy that they will leave your church and go elsewhere. This is not necessarily a bad thing. It is dishonest for a person to remain part of a worshipping community if that community is worshipping in a way that that person feels is wrong or at least not meaningful. An increasing number of women and men are realizing this, and if changes away from a sexist liturgy are not made soon, they will be the ones who will leave. Often a person who is extremely dissatisfied with a church's worship will show dissatisfaction with most of the other activities of the church and actually act as a divisive force within the community. Both for the good of the community and for that particular person, a change to another congregation more in keeping with that person's beliefs and practices is in order.

You must also be prepared to accept the fact that if you have really been successful in eliminating sexism in your worship and liberating your liturgy, you will suddenly discover that many women and men in your church are experiencing worship and the Christian faith on a newer and deeper lever than ever before. A new excitement should begin to sweep through your church as both men and women begin to discover the freeing power that is present when the old stereotypes of sex roles and the God concept are broken. You will also discover that new persons are coming to your church—attracted by its honesty, by its willingness to face one of the crucial issues of our day and do something concrete and positive about it. You'll begin to experience what the apostle Paul dreamed about when he said that there is neither Jew nor Gentile, slave nor free, male nor female, but all are one in Christ Jesus.

# Appendix A:
# A Listing of Nonsexist Hymns

Our criteria for choosing the hymns below was their nonsexist language. We made no attempt to screen hymns on any other basis, be it theology or musical style. We did choose only hymns that appeared in at least two of the hymnals. Therefore, in all of the hymnals, there are other nonsexist hymns that appear. We provide this list for you only as a starter. You should check your own hymnal and make your own list. We determined that a hymn had nonsexist language on the following basis:

1. No masculine words used generically such as "mankind," "brotherhood," "sons of God," and so forth.
2. No masculine references to God such as "Lord" or "Father" and no references to God's reign as a "kingdom."
3. No masculine references to Christ other than "he," "him," or "his."
4. No references to the Church or to objects as "she."

In preparing these charts we used several of the major Protestant denominations' most popular hymnals. We did not attempt to be inclusive, but merely representative, in choosing hymnals. If your denomination is not represented, you can make your own column for your hymnal. And whether or not your hymnal is listed, we encourage you as soon as you can to do your own chart.

| | *Baptist Hymnal* Southern Baptist American Baptist | *Christian Worship* Disciples of Christ American Baptist | *The Book of Hymns* United Methodist | *Pilgrim Hymnal* United Church of Christ | *Lutheran Book of Worship* Lutheran Church in America The American Lutheran Church The Evangelical Lutheran Church of Canada The Lutheran Church—Missouri Synod | *The Hymnal* United Presbyterian |
|---|---|---|---|---|---|---|
| Art Thou Weary | • | • | • | | | • |
| Author of Life Divine | | | • | | | • |
| Be Known to Us in Breaking Bread | • | | • | • | | • |
| Beneath the Cross of Jesus | • | • | • | • | • | • |
| Bread of the World in Mercy Broken | • | • | • | • | | • |
| Breathe on Me, Breath of God | • | | • | • | • | • |
| Christ, Whose Glory Fills the Skies | • | | • | • | • | • |
| Come Down, O Love Divine | | | • | • | • | |
| Come Let Us Tune Our Loftiest Song | • | | • | | | |
| Come, Ye Disconsolate | • | • | • | | | • |
| Fling Out the Banner | • | • | | • | | • |
| Go, Tell It on the Mountain | | | • | • | | |

| | Baptist Hymnal / Southern Baptist / American Baptist | Christian Worship / Disciples of Christ / American Baptist | The Book of Hymns / United Methodist | Pilgrim Hymnal / United Church of Christ | Lutheran Book of Worship / Lutheran Church in America / The American Lutheran Church / The Evangelical Lutheran Church of Canada / The Lutheran Church—Missouri Synod | The Hymnal / United Presbyterian |
|---|---|---|---|---|---|---|
| God, That Madest Earth and Heaven | ● | ● | ● | ● | ● [1] | ● |
| Guide Me, O Thou Great Jehovah | ● | ● | ● | ● | ● | ● |
| I Heard the Voice of Jesus Say | ● | ● | ● | | ● | ● |
| I Know That My Redeemer Lives | | ● | ● | | ● [2] | |
| I Look to Thee in Every Need | | | ● | ● | | ● |
| I Love to Tell the Story | ● | ● | ● | ● | | ● |
| In Heavenly Love Abiding | ● | ● | ● | ● | | ● |
| In the Cross of Christ I Glory | ● | ● | ● | ● | ● | ● |
| In the Hour of Trial | ● | ● | ● | ● | ● | ● |
| Jesus Calls Us O'er the Tumult | ● | ● | ● | ● | ● | ● |
| Jesus, Lover of My Soul | ● | ● | ● | ● | | ● |
| Jesus, Savior, Pilot Me | ● | ● | ● | ● | ● | ● |

[1] Has variant reading of third and fourth verses that is sexist.
[2] Has sexist variation in sixth verse.

| | *Baptist Hymnal* Southern Baptist American Baptist | *Christian Worship* Disciples of Christ American Baptist | *The Book of Hymns* United Methodist | *Pilgrim Hymnal* United Church of Christ | *Lutheran Book of Worship* Lutheran Church in America / The American Lutheran Church / The Evangelical Lutheran Church of Canada / The Lutheran Church—Missouri Synod | *The Hymnal* United Presbyterian |
|---|---|---|---|---|---|---|
| Jesus, Thy Boundless Love to Me | • | • | • | | • | • |
| Just As I Am | • | • | • | • | • | • |
| Lead, Kindly Light | • | • | • | • | | • |
| Love Divine, All Loves Excelling | • | • | • | • | • | • |
| More Love to Thee, O Christ | • | • | • | • | | • |
| Must Jesus Bear the Cross Alone | • | • | • | | | |
| My Faith Looks Up to Thee | • | • | • | • | • | • |
| My Hope is Built on Nothing Less | • | | • | | • | |
| Nearer, My God, to Thee | • | • | • | • | | • |
| Now the Day Is Over | • | • | • | • | •³ | • |
| O Grant Us Light That We May Know | | • | | | | • |
| O Love That Wilt Not Let Me Go | • | • | • | • | • | • |

³Has variant reading of sixth verse that is sexist.

| | Baptist Hymnal<br>Southern Baptist<br>American Baptist | Christian Worship<br>Disciples of Christ<br>American Baptist | The Book of Hymns<br>United Methodist | Pilgrim Hymnal<br>United Church of Christ | Lutheran Book of Worship<br>Lutheran Church in America<br>The American Lutheran Church<br>The Evangelical Lutheran Church of Canada<br>The Lutheran Church—Missouri Synod | The Hymnal<br>United Presbyterian |
|---|---|---|---|---|---|---|
| O Perfect Love, All Human Thought Transcending | ● | | ● | ● | ● | ● |
| O Sometimes the Shadows Are Deep | ● | | ● | | | |
| Open My Eyes, That I May See | ● | | ● | | | |
| Peace, Perfect Peace | | | ● | | | ● |
| Purer in Heart, O God | ● | ● | | | | |
| Rock of Ages, Cleft for Me | ● | ● | ● | ● | ● | ● |
| Sing Them Over Again to Me | ● | ● | ● | | | |
| Spirit Divine, Attend Our Prayers | ● | ● | ● | ● | | ● |
| Still, Still with Thee | ● | ● | ● | ● | | ● |
| There Is a Fountain Filled with Blood | ● | | ● | | | ● |
| This Is the Day of Light | | ● | | | | ● |
| Thou, Whose Unmeasured Temple Stands | | | ● | | | ● |
| We Are Climbing Jacob's Ladder | | | ● | | | |

# Appendix B:
# Guidelines for Nonsexist Use of Language in Worship

## Introduction

In the preparation of these guidelines we are especially indebted to the National Council of Teachers of English for their excellent "Guidelines for Nonsexist Use of Language in NCTE Publications." This complete set of guidelines is available from the National Council of Teachers of English, 1111 Kenyon Road, Urbana, IL 61801 (1–15 copies free; more than 15, 6¢ each prepaid). Ask for Stock No. 19719.

\* \* \*

"Sexism" is the use of words or actions that arbitrarily assign roles or characteristics to people on the basis of sex. Neither men nor women can reach full potential when they are trapped in stereotyped language and actions. We believe that sexist language relating to worship falls into two categories—language about people and language about God. We consider each separately.

## Language About People

I. "He/man" language as generic language about people should be avoided.

    A. Alternatives for nouns such as "mankind" and "brotherhood" must be found.

| Examples | Alternatives |
|---|---|
| 1. All *mankind* is one *brotherhood*. | All *humanity* is one *family*. All *people* are related. |

| | |
|---|---|
| 2. The *common man* does not think *he* is a great sinner. | *Ordinary people* do not think *they* are great sinners. |
| 3. We must elect a new *chairman* of the Administrative Board today. | We must elect a new *chair* (presiding officer) of the Administrative board today. |

B. Alternatives should be found for masculine pronouns when the person being referred to could be either male or female.

*Examples*  *Alternatives*

| | |
|---|---|
| 1. It is important that a Christian recognize that *he* is a sinner. | It is important that Christians recognize that *they* are sinners. |
| 2. The ordinary Christian is concerned about *his* future. | The ordinary Christian is concerned about the future. |
| 3. A Christian must follow *his* conscience when deciding such a complex ethical question. | As a Christian you must follow *your* conscience when deciding such a complex ethical question. |

C. Use plural pronouns to refer to an indefinite pronoun (*everybody, everyone, anybody, anyone*).

*Example*  *Alternative*

| | |
|---|---|
| Everyone who comes to church today should bring *his* Bible. | Everyone who comes to church today should bring *their* Bible. |

II. Language that demeans women should be eliminated.
   A. Parallel descriptions of men and women should be used.

*Examples*  *Alternatives*

| | |
|---|---|
| 1. The *lady preacher* was in charge. | The *preacher* was in charge. |
| 2. Officers for this year include John Jones, director of Jones & Smith Insurance, and Jill Adams, former Miss Illinois. | Officers for this year include John Jones, director of Jones & Smith Insurance, and Jill Adams, receptionist at Hill & Daughters. |

3. Reverend Lee and Mrs. Sing, who is also a minister, led our service.

Reverends Lee and Sing led our service. Reverends Sing and Lee led our service.

4. Mr. and Mrs. Ralph Green will be greeters at Sunday's service.

Mary Lou and Ralph Green will be greeters at Sunday's service. Or Ms. Mary and Mr. Ralph Green will be greeters at Sunday's service.

B. Terms that patronize or trivialize women or girls should be avoided; these include sexist suffixes and adjectives that depend on stereotyped masculine or feminine markers.

| *Examples* | *Alternatives* |
|---|---|
| 1. Salesgirl | Saleswoman |
| 2. Lady | Woman |
| 3. Libber | Feminist |
| 4. Coed | Student |
| 5. Priestess | Priest |
| 6. Man-sized job | Big job |
| 7. Old wives' tale | Superstitious belief |
| 8. Suffragette | Suffragist |

III. Sex-role stereotyping should be avoided.

*Examples*

*Alternatives*

1. Ministers work such long hours that they often neglect their wives and children.

Ministers work such long hours that they often neglect their families.

2. The group was led by women minister Sally Ryan.

The group was led by minister Sally Ryan.

3. The Sunday School teacher . . . she

The Sunday School teachers . . . they

4. The minister . . . he

Ministers . . . they

5. The ladies' aide society bustled about getting dinner for the group.

The women's society served dinner to the group.

## Language About God

I. Avoid masculine-only references for God.
   A. Use nongender titles or balance masculine and feminine ones.

| *Examples* | *Alternatives* |
|---|---|
| King | Ruler |
| Lord | Sovereign |
| Father | Creator |
| Master | Parent |
| | *Abba* |
| | King/Queen |
| | Mother/Father |

   B. Avoid the use of masculine-only pronouns for God. Repeat nouns, recast sentences, or balance masculine and feminine pronouns.

| *Examples* | *Alternatives* |
|---|---|
| God loves you. He cares for you. He will be with you always. | God loves you. God cares for you. *Yahweh* will be with you always. |
| | God loves you, cares for you, and will be with you always. |
| | God loves you. He cares for you. She will be with you always. |
| God himself cares for you. | God Godself cares for you. |
| | God himself/herself cares for you. |
| | God cares for you. |

II. Trinitarian Formula

    A. Try to avoid the use of the Trinitarian formula, or at least use alternative forms.

| *Example* | *Alternatives* |
|---|---|
| Father, Son, and Holy Spirit | God, Jesus (or the Christ or Jesus Christ), and Holy Spirit |
| | Creator, Redeemer, Sustainer |
| | Creator, Liberator, Advocate |
| | Maker, Jesus, Holy Spirit |
| | Creator, Savior, Healer |
| | Source, Servant, Guide |
| | Three in One, One in Three |

    B. The important thing about affirmations concerning Jesus as a "man" is not that he became male but that he became human.

| *Examples* | *Alternatives* |
|---|---|
| Jesus, the man | Jesus, the person |
| Jesus, Son of Man | Jesus, Child of Humanity (or Humanity's Child) |

    C. The word for the Holy Spirit in Hebrew is feminine and in Greek is neuter; thus accurate translations should use at least the pronoun "it," if not "she," when referring to the Holy Spirit.

| *Example* | *Alternatives* |
|---|---|
| The Holy Spirit . . . he will come . . . | The Holy Spirit . . . it will come . . . |
| | The Holy Spirit . . . she will come . . . |
| | The Holy Spirit will come . . . |

III. Try to discover as many nonsexual images for God as you can. They abound both in the Bible and in contemporary literature. *Examples:* Light, Rock, Glory, Truth, Love, Ground of Being, Fire, First and Last.

IV. To help people become more aware of the analogical character of all our language for God, it is helpful to restructure prayers and other liturgical formulations as similes rather than as metaphors.

| *Examples* | *Alternatives* |
|---|---|
| O Father, we pray for your help . . . | O God, who watches over us like a father, we pray for your help . . . |
| O Mother, we pray for your presence . . . | O God, who cares for us like a mother hovering over her young, we pray for your presence . . . |

V. If you do use sexual images for God, it is good to try to find some that go beyond our sexual stereotypes.

| *Examples* | *Alternatives* |
|---|---|
| God as a strong father | God as a man painting a beautiful picture |
| God as a nurturing mother | God as a woman searching for her coin |

VI. Alternatives need to be found for other descriptions of God's presence.

| *Example* | *Alternatives* |
|---|---|
| Kingdom of God | Realm of God<br>Reign of God<br>Rule of God |

# Appendix C: Suggested Reading and Other Resources

## Books

### On Sexist Language

Key, Mary Ritchie. *Male/Female Language*. Metuchen, NJ: Scarecrow Press, 1975.

Kramarae, Cheris. *Women and Men Speaking*. Rowley, MA: Newbury House Publishing, 1981.

Lakoff, Robin. *Language and Woman's Place*. New York: Harper & Row, 1975.

Miller, Casey, and Swift, Kate. *The Handbook of Nonsexist Writing*. New York: Lippincott and Crowell, 1980.

Miller, Casey, and Swift, Kate. *Words and Women*. Garden City, NY: Doubleday, Anchor Books, 1977.

Nilsen, Alleen Pace; Bosmajian, Haig; Gershuny, H. Lee; and Stanley, Julia P. *Sexism and Language*. Urbana, IL: National Council of Teachers of English, 1977.

Spender, Dale. *Man Made Language*. London: Routledge and Kegan Paul, 1980.

Thorne, Barrie, and Henley, Nancy, eds. *Language and Sex; Difference and Dominance*. Rowley, MA: Newbury House Publishing, 1975.

Thorne, Barrie; Kramarae, Cheris; and Henley, Nancy. *Language, Gender and Society*. Rowley, MA: Newbury House Publishing, 1983.

### On Sexist Language and Religion

Emswiler, Thomas Neufer, and Emswiler, Sharon Neufer. *Wholeness in Wor-

*ship—Creative Models for Sunday, Family, and Special Services.* New York: Harper & Row, 1980.

Engelsman, Joan Chamberlain. *The Feminine Dimension of the Divine.* Philadelphia: Westminster Press, 1979.

Mollenkott, Virginia Ramey. *Divine Feminine.* New York: Crossroads Pub., 1983.

Mollenkott, Virginia Ramey. *Women, Men and the Bible.* Nashville, TN: Abingdon, 1977.

Russell, Letty, ed. *The Liberating Word—A Guide to Non-Sexist Interpretation of the Bible.* Philadelphia: Westminster Press, 1976.

Russell, Letty M. *Becoming Human.* Philadelphia: Westminster Press, 1982.

Stone, Merlin. *When God Was a Woman.* New York: Harcourt Brace Jovanovich, 1976.

Trible, Phyllis. *God and the Rhetoric of Sexuality.* Philadelphia: Fortress Press, 1978.

Watkins, Keith. *Faithful and Fair—Transcending Sexist Language in Worship.* Nashville, TN: Abingdon, 1981.

## Bibles, Songbooks, Hymnals, and Worship Resource Books

Allen, Art. *Seeds of Hope.* Stuart, IA: Re-Creation Ministries, 1983.

*Because We Are One People.* Chicago, IL: Ecumenical Women's Center, 1974.

Cymbala, Michael A. *Gather to Remember.* Chicago: G.I.A. Publications, Inc., 1982.

Duck, Ruth C., ed. *Bread for the Journey—Resources for Worship.* New York: Pilgrim Press, 1981. Also available from the Wesley Foundation (211 N. School St., Normal, IL 61761), $3.95.

Duck, Ruth C., and Bausch, Michael G. *Everflowing Streams—Songs for Worship.* New York: Pilgrim Press, 1981. Also available from the Wesley Foundation (211 N. School St., Normal, IL 61761), $3.95.

Emswiler, Sharon Neufer, and Emswiler, Thomas Neufer, eds. *Sisters and Brothers, Sing!*, Second Edition. Normal, IL: The Wesley Foundation, 1977. Order from The Wesley Foundation, 211 N. School St., Normal, IL 61761. $3.50 plus 75¢ postage and handling.

Emswiler, Sharon Neufer, and Emswiler, Thomas Neufer, eds. *Put On Your Party Clothes.* Normal, IL: The Wesley Foundation, 1977. Order from address listed above; $2.00 plus 75¢ postage and handling.

Haugerud, Joann. *The Word for Us*. Seattle, WA: Coalition Task Force on Women and Religion, 1977. Order from Coalition Task Force on Women and Religion, 4759 15th Ave., N.E., Seattle, WA 98105, $5.95. This is a paraphrase of the Gospels of John and Mark, Epistles to the Romans and the Galatians in inclusive language.

*The Inclusive Language Lectionary*. Division of Education and Ministry, National Council of Churches of Christ in the U.S.A. Published for the Cooperative Publication by John Knox Press, Atlanta; Pilgrim Press, New York; Westminster Press, Philadelphia; 1983.

*Life Songs*. Trumansburg, NY: K & R Music, 1982. Also available from The Wesley Foundation (211 N. School St., Normal, IL 61761).

Lodge, Ann, comp. *Creation Sings*. Philadelphia: Geneva Press, 1979. Order from Curriculum Services UPCUSA, Box 868, William Penn Annex, Philadelphia, PA 19105. $1.25.

Piccard, Kathyrn Ann. *Non-Sexist Hymn Concert Handbook*. Syracuse, NY: Episcopal Women's Action, 1982. Order from Episcopal Women's Caucus, 819 Madison St., Syracuse, NY 13210. $4.00

Rose, Steve. *A New Hymnal*. Stockbridge, MA: Persephone Music, 1980. Order from Persephone Music, Box 249, Stockbridge, MA 01262. $8.00. Also available from The Wesley Foundation (211 N. School St., Normal, IL 61761).

Stanton, Elizabeth Cady, and the Revising Committee. *The Woman's Bible*. Arno Press, 1972. Reprint of 1895 edition (two volumes in one). $16.00. Also available in paperback from Coalition Task Force on Women and Religion, 4759 15th Ave., N.E., Seattle, WA 98105. $6.95.

*Supplement to the Book of Hymns*. Nashville: The United Methodist Publishing House, 1982.

### Films

"Anything You Want to Be," Audio-Visual Education Center, University of Michigan, 416 Fourth Street, Ann Arbor, MI.

"Included Out"—a two-minute, 16mm color film by Sharon Neufer Emswiler. A humorous treatment of masculine generic language as commonly used in worship services. Order from Mass Media Ministries, 2116 N. Charles St., Baltimore, MD 21218.

"The Vision"—a two-minute, 16mm color film produced by Sharon and Tom Neufer Emswiler. A humorous treatment of the need to expand our God language to include the feminine. Also available from Mass Media Industries (see above).

## Periodical

*Women and Language News*, edited by Cheris Kramarae and Paula A. Treichler; asst. ed., Karen Lee Cole. Published three times a year. U.S. Subscription $5 a year. Order from University of Illinois at Urbana-Champaign, 244 Lincoln Hall, 702 South Wright Street, Urbana, IL 61801.

## Articles and Pamphlets

The Community Council, Wesley Theological Seminary, Washington, D.C. "Toward More Inclusive Language in the Worship of the Church—A Position Statement," January, 1980. Order from Bookstore, Wesley Theological Seminary, Washington, D.C. 20016. 25¢.

Dart, John. "Balancing Out the Trinity: The Genders of the Godhead." *The Christian Century*, February 16–23, 1983, pp. 147–150.

Eighth Day Center for Justice. "Cleaning Up Sexist Language." 1980. Order from Eighth Day Center for Justice, 22 East Van Buren Street, Chicago, IL 60605.

Emswiler, Sharon Neufer, and Emswiler, Tom Neufer. "Liturgy that includes Everyone." *In God's Image—Toward Wholeness for Women and Men*. Division for Mission in North America, Lutheran Church in America, 1976, pp. 10–12.

"Expanding Our Language About Humanity," 1977. Order from Church Leadership Resources, Box 179, St. Louis, MO 63166. 25¢.

Hoppin, Ruth. "Games Bible Translators Play." Women and Religion, a packet of educational materials by The National Organization for Women, Ecumenical Task Force on Women and Religion, 1957 East 73rd St., Chicago, Illinois, or Ruth Hoppin, 25 Portola Ave., Daly City, CA 94105.

Luecke, Jane Marie, O.S.B. "The Dominance Syndrome." *The Christian Century*, April 27, 1977, pp. 405–407.

Mollenkott, Virginia Ramey. "An Evangelical Feminist Confronts the Goddess." *The Christian Century*, October 20, 1982, pp. 1043–1046.

Soelle, Dorothee. "Mysticism, Liberation and the Names of God." *Christianity and Crisis*, June 22, 1981, pp. 179–185.

The Task Force on Women, Presbytery of the Twin Cities Area. "A Guide to Inclusive Church Language." Second Edition, June, 1979. Order from Task Force on Women, Presbytery of the Twin Cities Area, 122 W. Franklin, Minneapolis, MN 55408. 75¢.

Tennis, Diane. "The Loss of the Father God—Why Women Rage and Grieve." *Christianity and Crisis*, June 8, 1981, pp. 164–170.

Turner, Rosa Shand. "The Increasingly Visible Female and the Need for Generic Terms." *The Christian Century*, March 16, 1977, pp. 248–252.

Wentz, Frederick K. "Inclusive Language to Proclaim an Inclusive Gospel." *In God's Image—Toward Wholeness for Women and Men*. Division for Mission in North America, Lutheran Church in America, 1976, pp. 8–9.

White, James F. "Justice and the Work of Liturgical Renewal." *Christianity and Crisis*, June 9, 1980, pp. 173–177.

Withers, Barbara A., ed. *Language About God in Liturgy and Scripture—A Study Guide*. Philadelphia: Geneva Press, 1980.